TBap T1's Dining Table

티밥, T1의 밥상

TChef's TBap Tier List for T1

T1을 위한 티셰프의 티밥 티어리스트

GOLDEN RABBIT

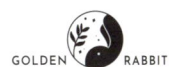

Tier List for T1

Foreword

Five years have already passed since I joined T1. T1 is a legendary team, a globally renowned organization that has claimed victory at the League of Legends World Championship—commonly known as Worlds—five times and is home to some of the world's best players.
Over the years, I've had the privilege of meeting many players. Despite their young age, I was deeply moved by their incredible passion and professionalism, and I've learned so much from them. I wanted to bring some comfort to the hearts of parents worried about their children and approached every meal I prepared with the care of a family member, thinking of all the staff and players at T1 as my own.
This cookbook contains recipes and stories behind the meals filled with cherished memories from my time at T1. I hope to share these with everyone who has supported and loved T1.

T1과 함께한 시간, 벌써 5년이 흘렀습니다.
T1은 롤드컵에서 총 5번의 우승을 차지한 세계적인 명문 구단으로서 최고의 선수들을 보유한 전설적인 팀입니다. 이 기간 동안 다양한 선수들을 만났습니다. 비록 어린 나이지만 그들의 놀라운 열정과 프로 의식에 깊은 감동을 받았고 많은 것을 배웠습니다. 자식을 걱정하시는 부모님의 마음을 조금이나마 위로하고 싶었고, 가족 같은 마음으로 T1의 모든 임직원과 선수단을 생각하며 식사를 준비했습니다. T1에서의 소중한 추억이 담긴 음식들의 레시피와 에피소드를 이 책에 담아 T1을 사랑해주신 모든 분과 나누고자 합니다.

T1 Chef, Alex Kim(김재형)
@moneysay48
@t1_bap

A chef who has devoted his youth entirely to his passion for cooking. He began his culinary journey as a military cook, preparing meals three times a day for 800 people. From sizzling fried rice on a teppan to Spanish dishes, pasta, and omelet rice, he honed his craft across a variety of restaurants before serving as a chef in hotels, hospitals, universities, and department stores. Proud of the countless recipes he has developed along the way, he now shoulders the responsibility of keeping the T1 family healthy as their dedicated "TChef(T1's Chef)." Even today, he still spends his nights immersed in both League of Legends and new culinary experiments.

요리에 대한 열정으로 젊음을 아낌없이 투자한 요리에 진심인 셰프. 하루 세 번 800명의 끼니를 담당하는 취사병으로 요리에 입문했다. 철판 볶음밥부터 스페인 음식, 파스타, 오므라이스 전문점을 거쳐 호텔, 병원, 대학교, 백화점에서 셰프로 활약했다. 그동안 직접 개발한 수많은 요리를 자부심으로 삼아 T1 식구의 건강을 책임지는 티셰프로서 활약하고 있다. 지금도 밤마다 LoL과 요리 연구를 즐긴다.

Contents

Episode 01 — 12

Tteokguk
떡국

BoxeR
박서(임요환)

Episode 02 — 24

King Tiger Shrimp Garlic Cheese Bake & Pork Neck Steak
킹타이거 갈릭치즈 구이 & 목살 스테이크

Episode 03 — 44

Rest Area Soul Food
휴게소 소울 푸드

Episode 04 — 68

Samgyetang
삼계탕

Gumayusi
구마유시(이민형)

Episode 05

Paella & Rib Barbecue

빠에야 & 립 바베큐

78

Episode 06

Buncha & Banh Mi

분짜 & 반미

102

Episode 07

Malatang & Jisamsun

마라탕 & 지삼선

Faker
페이커(이상혁)

122

Episode 08

Tenderloin Steak & Ragu Pasta

안심 스테이크 & 라구 파스타

Bang & Wolf
뱅 & 울프(배준식 & 이재완)

142

Episode 09 — 164

Jangeodeopbap

장어덮밥

Doran
도란(최현준)

Episode 10 — 176

Feijoada & Moqueca

페이조아다 & 모케카

Episode 11 — 196

Wanggalbitang

왕갈비탕

Episode 12 — 210

Hamburg Steak

함박 스테이크

Episode 13

American Hot Dog

핫도그

222

Episode 14

Jeukseoktteokbokki

즉석떡볶이

234

Episode 15

Cheese Tonkatsu

치즈돈까스

244

Untara
운타라(박의진)

The English names for Korean cuisine follow the "Foreign Language Notation of Korean Food Menus" published by www.hansik.or.kr.

한식 요리의 영어 표기는 www.hansik.or.kr의 '한식메뉴 외국어 표기법'을 따랐습니다.

Episode 01

Tteokguk

Lim Yo-hwan's Lunar New Year Cooking Class

떡국 – 설날, 임요환의 요리 교실

Date	Feb 12, 2021
Introduction	Let's try the tteokguk made by Lim Yo-hwan, the Terran Emperor and legend of T1.
Allergen Information	Egg, Beef
Spiciness Level	Mild
Way to Cook	Boiling

일자	2021. 2. 12
소개	T1의 레전드, 황제 테란 임요환 선수가 직접 만든 떡국을 맛봅시다.
알러지 정보	계란, 소고기
맵기 단계	순한맛
조리 기법	끓이기

STORY

"Hello everyone, I'm Lim Yo-hwan. Today, I'm planning to make some tteokguk for our hardworking T1 players."
Lim Yo-hwan, the legendary "Emperor of Terran" from StarCraft, made tteokguk.
T1 is a joint venture between South Korea's SK Telecom and the U.S. company Comcast. "SK Telecom T1" was founded in 2004 with Lim Yo-Hwan at its core. Later, in 2019, Comcast joined as a co-owner. As a founding member, Lim Yo-Hwan laid the foundation for T1, and, along with Faker, holds the title of "T1 Legend".

"여러분 안녕하세요? 임요환입니다. 오늘은 고생하고 있는 우리 T1 선수들을 위해 설날 떡국을 만들어볼 생각입니다."
스타크래프트 '테란의 황제'이자 레전드인 임요환 선수가 떡국을 끓였다.
T1은 대한민국 기업 SK텔레콤과 미국 기업 컴캐스트의 합작 회사다. 2004년 임요환 선수를 중심으로 'SK텔레콤 T1'이 창단되었다. 이후 2019년에는 컴캐스트가 공동주주로 참여하여 현재의 T1이 되었다. 임요환 선수는 T1의 창단 멤버로서 팀의 초석을 다졌으며 실제로 페이커와 함께 'T1 레전드' 호칭을 갖고 있다.

So it is truly an honor that Lim Yo-hwan personally prepared this tteokguk. The filming process went as follows: I had previously recorded a cooking video for tteokguk with the T1 content team. Lim Yo-hwan then followed the video on a monitor, carefully replicating each step to perfection.
While I had to film the video for him to follow, I was somewhat unfamiliar with the process, as I'm part of T1 but not a player.

그런 임요환 선수가 손수 끓여주신 떡국이라니! 영광스러운 일이 아닐 수 없다.
해당 영상의 촬영 방식은 이러했다. 사전에 T1 콘텐츠팀과 내가 먼저 찍어놓은 떡국 요리 영상을 보고 모니터로 보면서 따라 해 음식을 완성해나가는 방식이다.
내가 먼저 영상을 찍어야 했다. 나는 T1에 몸담고 있기는 하지만 선수단이 아니라서 촬영에 낯설었다. 마치 TV나 유튜브에 나오는 유명인처럼 능수능란해 보여야겠다는 생각이 들었다.

Lim 'BoxeR' Yo-hwan
'박서' 임요환

I knew I needed to come across as polished and professional, much like the well-known personalities you see on TV or YouTube, to make it easier for Lim Yo-hwan to follow along. "I'm a cooking YouTuber, I'm a cooking YouTuber," I repeated to myself in a playful manner hundreds of times as we continued filming. It was both satisfying and surreal to watch Lim Yo-hwan follow the video and cook along.
First, he boiled the water and added the beef bone extract. Since this tteokguk is paired with baechugeotjeori as a side dish, he had to make that too.

그래야 임요환 선수도 잘 따라 할 테니까! "나는 요리 유튜버다, 나는 요리 유튜버다" 몇 백 번 되뇌며 능청스럽게 촬영을 이어갔다.
그렇게 찍은 영상을 임요환 선수가 보면서 요리하는 걸 보니 뿌듯하고 신기했다.
먼저 물을 올리시고 사골 엑기스를 투입! 떡국과 겉절이 조합이라, 배추 겉절이까지 만들어야 한다. 임요환 선수는 미리 찍어둔 영상을 되돌려보면서 열중했다.
중간에 내가 투입되어 응원해드리는 사이 대망의 완성!

Lim Yo-hwan diligently followed the video, even rewinding it at times. Finally, the dish was complete! I tasted the tteokguk and kimchi right away, and the seasoning was perfect. It was a bit surprising—after all, this was a master's touch, the same precision he used in his gaming days!

That day, the players and staffs experienced a truly special event, which might even be considered historic. I'm incredibly grateful to the content team and to Lim Yo-hwan for making this all happen.

About the Dish

Tteokguk is a meaningful dish in Korea's traditional New Year's celebration, symbolizing wishes for family health and good fortune. It's also considered a way of symbolically adding a year to one's age. While this version uses beef broth as a base, it can also be made with anchovy or beef bone broth. The dish has evolved to include variations like pollack roe tteokguk or tteokguk with joraengitteok(snowman-shaped rice cake), catering to different preferences.

나는 제일 먼저 떡국과 겉절이의 간을 맛보았다. 간이 너무 딱 맞아서 살짝 놀랐다. 역시 마우스 컨트롤을 자유자재로 하던 손맛이다?!
이날 선수들과 임직원이 어떻게 보면 역사적일 수도 있는 특별한 이벤트를 경험을 할 수 있었다. 자리를 마련해준 콘텐츠팀과 직접 참여해주신 임요환 선수께 감사하고 감사하다!

음식 소개

떡국은 한국의 고유 명절인 설날에 가족의 건강과 행운을 기원하는 음식이다. 한 살 더 먹는 의미로도 여겨지는 음식이다. 여기서는 소고기 국물을 베이스로 떡국을 만들지만, 멸치 육수나 사골 국물을 이용해도 된다. 명란을 넣은 명란떡국, 조랭이떡을 사용한 조랭이떡국 등 다양한 기호에 맞춰 다채롭게 변화하고 있다.

RECIPE

Ingredients (for 4 Servings)

Tteok : 400g
Beef : 100g
Eggs : 2
Green Onion : 50g

Broth

Water : 10 cups
Korean Soy Sauce : 2 tbsps
Sesame Oil : 1 tbsp
Cooking Oil : 1 tbsp
Fine Sea Salt(adjust to taste) : 1 tsp
Black Pepper : 1 tsp
Tuna Fish Sauce : 1 tbsp
Minced Garlic : 1 tbsp

Tool

Soup Bowl

Tip

- To make tteokguk more easily, you can use ground beef or pre-sliced beef.
- Store-bought bone broth is a convenient alternative for the base.
- If you don't have tteok, penne or rigatoni pasta works as a substitute.
- Making egg strips and adding them on top is also delicious.
- Pairing it with baechugeotjeori creates an amazing flavor combination.

재료 (4인분)

떡국떡 400g
소고기 100g
달걀 2개
대파 50g

육수

물 10컵
국간장 2큰술(한국 간장)
참기름 1큰술
식용유 1큰술
꽃소금 1작은술(기호에 맞게)
후추 1작은술
참치액 1작은술
다진 마늘 1큰술

도구

면기

- 떡국을 더 간편하게 먹고 싶을 땐 다진 소고기 또는 채썬 소고기를 사용해도 된다.
- 시판 사골육수를 넣고 간단하게 끓여 먹을 수도 있다.
- 떡이 없을 땐 펜네 또는 리가토니 파스타로 대체할 수 있다.
- 계란 지단을 만들어 올려도 맛있다.
- 배추겉절이랑 먹으면 환상의 꿀맛!

PREPARATION

1 Cut the beef into pieces about 2cm in size.

소고기를 2cm 정도 크기로 썰어준다.

2 Slice the green onion into thin pieces, about 0.2cm thick.

대파를 0.2cm 두께로 썰어준다.

COOKING STEPS

1 Soak the tteok in cold water for 20~30 minutes.

떡을 찬 물에 20~30분 담가서 불려준다.

2 Add sesame oil and cooking oil to the pan in a 1:1 ratio and heat over low heat.

팬에 참기름과 식용유를 1:1로 넣고 약불로 달군다.

3 Place the beef in a heated pan and stir-fry it over medium heat until the exterior is no longer red.

달군 팬에 소고기를 올리고 중간불로 겉면에 붉은색이 띄지 않도록 볶아준다.

4 Once the beef is cooked to a certain extent, pour water and boil over low heat for about 15 minutes.

소고기가 어느 정도 익으면 물을 부은 후 끓어오르면 약불로 15분간 끓인다.

5 Add the soaked tteok to the soup and continue boiling.

이 국물에 미리 불린 떡을 넣고 강불에서 끓인다.

6. When the tteok begins to float, add soy sauce and minced garlic. Bring it to a boil again, then taste and adjust the seasoning with fine sea salt if needed.

   떡이 떠오르면 국간장과 다진 마늘을 넣고 한 번 더 끓이고 나서 간을 본 후 모자란 간을 꽃소금으로 맞춘다.

7. Beat the eggs in advance, and once the tteok is mostly cooked, add the eggs and gently stir.

   미리 달걀을 풀어놓고 어느 정도 떡이 익은 걸 확인한 이후에 달걀을 넣고 저어준다.

8. Finally, add the green onion, sprinkle it with pepper, and carefully place it in a bowl.

   마지막으로 대파를 넣고 후추를 뿌리고 그릇에 조심스럽게 담는다.

Episode 02

King Tiger Shrimp Garlic Cheese Bake

& Pork Neck Steak

Filming Shorts and Dubbing

킹타이거새우 갈릭치즈 구이 & 돼지 목살 스테이크
- 숏츠 촬영하고 더빙하고

Date — Aug 10, 2021

Introduction — A special meal for our T1 players and staff to celebrate malbok—along with a T1 Shorts shoot?

일자 — 2021. 8. 10
소개 — 말복을 맞이해 지친 우리 T1 선수단과 임직원을 위한 특식에, T1숏츠 촬영까지?

STORY

I planned a special meal featuring king tiger shrimp, which had become a hot topic on social media due to its impressive size, to present to the entire T1 family. Adding the pork neck steak I had tasted during a trip to Vietnam seemed like the perfect complement to this special feast.

Then, the content team made an interesting suggestion—introduce the cooking process via YouTube Shorts to entertain the fans. Recalling the fun we had filming with Lim Yo-hwan previously, I immediately agreed. Before serving the special meal to the players, we filmed the Shorts. We captured every step—cleaning and grilling the shrimp to marinating and cooking the pork neck steak. The chefs also sampled the dishes during filming. The shrimp meat, as rich and mild as lobster, blended beautifully with the savory taste of cheese and the subtle aroma of butter.

SNS에서 화제였던 압도적인 크기의 킹타이거새우를 모든 T1 가족에게 선보이는 특식을 기획했다. 베트남 여행 중 맛봤던 돼지 목살 스테이크까지 곁들이면 완벽한 특별 만찬이 될 것 같았다.

그러던 중 콘텐츠팀에서 흥미로운 제안이 들어왔다. 유튜브 쇼츠로 음식 만드는 과정을 소개해 팬들에게 재미를 선사하자는 것. 임요환 선수와 함께 찍었던 이전 영상의 재미를 떠올리며 즉석에서 승낙했다. 선수들에게 특식을 제공하기 전에 쇼츠 촬영을 진행했다. 새우 손질부터 굽기, 돼지 목살 스테이크 양념과 조리 과정까지 모든 순간을 카메라에 담았다. 촬영 중 셰프들의 시식도 함께 이어졌다. 랍스터만큼 풍성하고 담백한 새우 살에 치즈의 고소함과 버터의 은은한 향기가 어우러졌다.

The tender pork neck steak, with its robust meaty flavor and the tangy hint of lemon, created a wonderful harmony.
After finishing the voice dubbing, we completed a natural Shorts video. "Today, we've prepared king tiger shrimp garlic cheese bake and pork neck steak for you all."
Once filming was done, the real event remained—serving the meal at the perfect time to live up to its name of special meal. Maintaining the warmth and flavor of the food and delivering it at its peak timing was most important. Preparing it in advance would diminish its taste. Fortunately, the players' schedule was surprisingly consistent. Every team arrived at the set time when the elevator doors opened. You could tell which team it was just by hearing the elevator chime. Mission accomplished!

부드러운 돼지 목살 스테이크의 풍부한 육향과 새콤한 레몬맛이 멋진 하모니를 선사했다.
목소리 더빙까지 마치며 자연스러운 쇼츠 영상을 완성했다. "오늘은 여러분을 위해 킹타이거새우 갈릭치즈 구이와 돼지 목살 스테이크를 준비했습니다."
촬영을 마치고 나니 특식이라는 이름에 걸맞는 맛을 제공하는 본선이 남아 있었다. 음식의 온기와 맛을 그대로 유지하며 최적의 타이밍에 요리를 내는 것이 가장 중요했다. 미리 만들어두면 맛이 덜하기 때문이다.
다행히도 선수단의 일정은 놀랍도록 규칙적이었다. 항상 정해진 시각에 엘리베이터 문이 열리고 각 팀이 들어왔다. 엘리베이터 문이 열리는 소리만 들어도 어느 팀인지 알 수 있을 정도였다. 그덕분에 미션 클리어!

The colossal size of the king tiger shrimp meant it wasn't cheap, but just seeing everyone's happy smiles and watching them enjoy the meal made it all worth it!

킹타이거새우는 어마어마한 크기만큼 가격도 만만치 않았지만, 모든 이의 행복한 미소와 즐거운 식사 모습을 보는 것만으로 입가에 미소가 가득 찼다!

🍴 About the Dish

King tiger shrimp garlic cheese bake is an impressive dish that combines large king tiger shrimp with garlic and cheese. After cleaning the shells and removing the innards, spread garlic butter on the shrimp, then top generously with mozzarella or parmesan cheese before baking. The result is shrimp meat that's rich and springy, similar to lobster, perfectly complementing the savory cheese. A sprinkle of parsley or a squeeze of lemon juice adds a fresh, aromatic touch. Serve it with a simple salad or bread for a splendid meal.

Pork neck steak is prepared by slicing the pork neck—a cut with a good balance of fat and lean meat—into thick pieces and grilling them to perfection. Thanks to its natural marbling, the steak remains tender and juicy. Simply season with salt, pepper, and herbs before grilling for a delicious result. Serving it with grilled garlic or vegetables makes for an even more satisfying meal.

음식 소개

킹타이거새우 갈릭치즈 구이는 거대한 킹타이거새우를 마늘과 치즈로 맛을 낸 화려한 요리다. 껍데기와 내장을 깔끔히 손질한 새우에 갈릭 버터를 바르고, 위에 모짜렐라나 파르메산 치즈를 듬뿍 올려 구워내면 랍스터처럼 풍부하고 탱글한 새우 살과 고소한 치즈가 완벽하게 어우러진다. 여기에 파슬리나 레몬즙을 곁들이면 감칠맛과 향이 살아나며, 간단한 샐러드나 빵과 함께 내면 근사한 한 끼 식사가 완성된다.

돼지 목살 스테이크는 지방과 살코기가 적절히 섞인 돼지 목살을 두툼하게 썰어 구워낸 요리다. 적당한 마블링 덕분에 부드러운 식감과 풍부한 육즙을 즐길 수 있으며, 소금·후추와 허브로 간단히 시즈닝해 구워도 맛이 뛰어나다. 구운 마늘이나 야채를 곁들이면 더욱 풍성한 한 끼가 완성된다.

RECIPE

 Ingredients
King Tiger Shrimp : 3
Mozzarella : 4 tbsps

 Garlic Sauce
Butter : 100g
Salt : 2g
Minced Garlic : 2 tbsps
Parsley : 1g
Olive Oil : 30ml
Lemon : 1

 Tool
Plate

 Tip
- If you want spiciness, you can add Cheongyang peppers or peperoncino powder to the sauce.
- By adding shrimp heads, chicken stock, a little pasta water, and pasta noodles to the oil used to cook the shrimp, you can make a savory shrimp pasta.
- Instead of using a pan, you can use an oven. In that case, season with salt and pepper, apply the sauce, sprinkle cheese and parsley, and then bake in a preheated oven at 200℃ for about 20 minutes.

 재료
킹타이거새우 3마리
모짜렐라치즈 4큰술

갈릭소스
버터 100g
소금 2g
다진 마늘 2큰술
파슬리 1g
올리브오일 30ml
레몬 1개

도구
접시

- 매콤함을 원한다면 소스에 청양고추나 페페론치노 가루를 추가하면 된다.
- 새우를 구운 오일에 새우 머리와 치킨 스톡과 면수를 조금 넣고 파스타면을 넣으면 감칠맛 나는 새우 파스타가 된다.
- 프라이팬 대신 오븐을 이용해도 된다. 소금과 후추를 뿌린 후 소스를 바르고 치즈, 파슬리까지 뿌리고 예열한 오븐에서 200도로 20분간 구우면 된다.

PREPARATION

1 **King Tiger Shrimp**

Remove the rostrum, antennae, legs, and telson from the shrimp.

킹타이거새우

새우 머리쪽 뿔, 수염, 다리, 꼬리 쪽 물주머니를 제거한다.

2 Bend the back and remove the innards with a toothpick.

등을 구부린 후 이쑤시개로 내장을 제거한다.

3 Make a slit along the back with a knife.

등에 칼집을 낸다.

4 Rinse and sprinkle with salt, and lemon juice.

세척하고 소금, 레몬즙을 뿌린다.

5 Garlic Sauce

Mix butter, salt, minced garlic, parsley, olive oil, and lemon juice together until well combined.

갈릭소스

버터, 소금, 다진 마늘, 파슬리, 올리브오일, 레몬즙을 잘 섞는다.

COOKING STEPS

1 After preparing the shrimp, melt butter in a preheated pan over medium heat and start cooking the scored side first.

손질된 새우를 예열된 팬에 중불로 버터를 녹인 후 칼집낸 면부터 굽기 시작한다.

2 Cook the shrimp over medium heat for about 3 minutes, then flip them to cook the other side. Since the shrimp may not stay flat on the grill, press them down gently with a spatula as they cook.

중불로 3분가량 새우를 굽고 나서 뒤집어서 굽는다. 이때, 새우 뒷면을 주걱으로 눌려주면서 구워준다.

③ After 2 minutes, flip them once more and cook the shrimp meat for about 1 minute. You can cook the shrimp heads with a torch for quicker preparation.

2분 후 한 번 더 뒤집어서 1분간 구워준다. 새우 머리를 토치로 구우면 더 빠르게 조리할 수 있다.

④ Flip them again and evenly coat with the pre-made sauce. Then sprinkle cheese on top, cover the pan, and cook for 3 minutes.

다시 뒤집어 미리 만들어놓은 소스를 골고루 발라준 후에, 그 위에 치즈를 뿌리고 뚜껑을 닫고 3분간 구워준다.

⑤ Once the cheese has fully melted, transfer the shrimp to a plate, sprinkle with parsley, and serve.

치즈가 잘 녹았으면 그릇에 옮기고 파슬리를 뿌린 후 플레이팅한다.

Cook 02

Pork Neck Steak

돼지 목살 스테이크

Allergen Information	Spiciness Level	Way to Cook
 Pork	 Mild	 Pan frying
알러지 정보 돼지고기	맵기 단계 순한맛	조리 기법 팬 프라잉

RECIPE

 Ingredients
Pork Neck : 300g
Whole Garlic : 8
Rosemary : a little

재료
돼지 목살 300g
통마늘 8개
로즈마리 약간

 Sauce
Soy Sauce : 2 tbsps
Sugar : 2 tbsps
Lemon Juice : 10ml
Garlic : 2 tbsps
Pepper : 0.5 tsp
Sesame Oil : 1 tbsp
Cooking Oil : 1 tbsp
Coriander Powder : 0.2 tsp
Chicken Powder : 0.2 tsp
Beef Powder : 0.2 tsp
Bay Leaves : 4
Cooking Oil : 30ml

양념장
간장 2큰술
설탕 2큰술
레몬즙 10ml
마늘 2큰술
후추 0.5작은술
참기름 1큰술
식용유 1큰술
코리앤더 파우더 0.2작은술
치킨 파우더 0.2작은술
비프 파우더 0.2작은술
월계수잎 4
식용유 30ml

 Tip
- Pork neck steak makes a fantastic burger or sandwich when served on hamburger buns or toast with whole grain mustard.
- Adding butter can enhance the flavor!
- It also makes a great steak salad when served with salad greens, bocconcini cheese, and hot sauce.
- You can also marinate chicken or beef in the sauce for different steak variations, each with its own unique flavor.

- 햄버거빵이나 식빵에 돼지 목살 스테이크와 홀그레인 머스터드를 추가해서 먹으면 훌륭한 버거와 샌드위치가 된다.
- 버터를 추가하면 풍미를 살릴 수 있다.
- 샐러드, 보코치니치즈, 핫소스와 곁들여도 잘 어울리는 스테이크 샐러드가 된다.
- 목살 이외도 닭고기, 소고기에 소스를 재워도 각기 재료마다 특징이 다른 스테이크가 된다.

PREPARATION

1 Sauce

Add all the ingredients used for the marinade together and stir well to ensure they are well mixed.

양념장

양념에 사용할 재료를 모두 한데 넣고 잘 섞이도록 저어준다.

2 Pork Neck

Remove the blood from the pork neck using a kitchen towel.

돼지 목살

키친타월로 목살의 핏물을 제거한다.

③ Prick it all over with a fork.

포크로 콕콕 찔러준다.

④ Marinate the pork neck in the prepared sauce for about 1 hour.

미리 준비한 소스에 목살을 1시간 정도 재운다.

COOKING STEPS

1 Add cooking oil to the pan and heat over medium heat, then place the marinated pork neck on the pan.

팬에 식용유를 두르고, 중간불로 예열을 먼저 한 후 재웠던 목살을 얹는다.

2 After about 1 minute, reduce the heat to low and flip the pork neck.

1분 후 약불로 바꾸고 목살을 뒤집는다.

③ Remove the pork neck from the pan and grill the whole garlic cloves.

목살을 덜어내고 통마늘을 굽는다.

④ Plate the shrimp and steak on a single plate.

새우와 스테이크를 한 접시에 플레이팅한다.

Episode 03

Rest Area Soul Food

Date	Nov 5, 2020
Introduction	Let's experience the travel vibes we missed because of COVID! How about we take a trip to the rest area with our food?
일자	2020. 11. 5
소개	코로나 때문에 못간 여행 기분을 느껴보자! 음식으로 휴게소나 가볼까?

STORY

During the COVID-19 pandemic, which now feels like a distant past, news of someone on the team or in the staff testing positive seemed to come in daily. "Who will cook for my family if I catch COVID!" Driven by the responsibility to ensure the meals and health of the T1 family, the chefs and I were particularly vigilant about our health. The culinary team voluntarily conducted tests three times a week using self-diagnostic kits. Each time, we would chant to ourselves, "Negative, please be negative," as if casting a magic spell.

이제는 아주 먼 과거처럼 느껴지는 코로나 팬데믹 시절, 선수단과 임직원 사이에서 누군가가 확진이라는 소식이 매일 같이 들려왔다.
"내가 코로나에 걸리면 우리 식구들 밥은 누가 해주나!" T1 가족의 식사와 건강을 책임져야 한다는 책임감에 나를 비롯한 셰프들은 각별히 건강에 신경을 썼다. 그래서 셰프진은 일주일에 세 번씩 자가진단 키트를 사용해 자발적으로 검사를 시행했다. 그때마다 "음성, 제발 음성" 마법의 주문을 외웠다.

One day, as I was checking on whether we had enough side dishes, I had a brief conversation with a staff member. "I really want to travel. I miss the sotteoksotteok we used to eat at rest areas, and I want to have some udon too." Upon hearing that, I thought to myself, "Will that day ever come? Even if it does, it will be in the distant future…" Contrary to my thoughts, I found myself saying, "Then, I'll send you some rest area food next week!" We both stared blankly at each other, wondering what that meant. So, the next week's menu was set: rest area's popular snacks. Deciding on rest area food brought back fleeting memories of freely traveling and enjoying delicious meals. It made me eagerly anticipate the day when that would come back.

하루는 평소처럼 반찬이 부족하지 않은지 둘러보던 중 한 직원과 잠시 대화를 나누게 되었다. "여행을 가고 싶어요. 휴게소에서 먹던 소떡소떡도 먹고 싶고, 우동도 먹고 싶어요", 그의 말에 '그런 날이 언제나 올까? 오더라도 먼 훗날일 거야…'라는 생각이 스쳤다. 생각과 달리 나도 모르게 "그럼, 다음 주에 휴게소 음식을 보내드릴게요!"라는 말을 내뱉어버렸다. 서로 눈만 멀뚱멀뚱 이건 무슨 소리?!
그렇게 다음 주 메뉴는 휴게소 국민 간식으로 정해져버렸다. 휴게소 음식으로 정하고 나니 자유롭게 여행을 떠나고, 맛있는 음식을 즐기던 그 시절 장면이 떠올랐다. 즐거운 상상으로 하루 빨리 그날이 오길 손꼽아 기다리게 되었다.

Finally, D-Day arrived. When the best rest area menus like kkomagimbap, butter ojingeogui, tteokbokki, butter-roasted potatoes, sotteoksotteok, and fish cakes were served, the once-stiff and awkward lunch hour was filled with smiles of joy. The sight of smiling eyes above the masks! My shoulders lifted, and my heart warmed.

드디어 D-Day. 꼬마김밥, 버터오징어, 떡볶이, 버터감자구이, 소떡소떡, 어묵바 등 휴게소 베스트 메뉴들이 등장하자, 조심스럽고 서먹하던 점심 식사 시간이 반가움의 미소로 가득 찼다. 마스크 위로 보이는 웃는 눈빛이라니! 어깨가 으쓱, 가슴이 따뜻해졌다.

About the Dish

Kkomagimbap is a convenient food made much smaller than regular gimbap, allowing you to enjoy a bite-sized portion. It can be easily made with basic ingredients such as pickled radish, burdock, carrot, and egg strips, and various flavors are created by changing the fillings, such as spicy stir-fried fish cake or tuna mayo. It is popular as a snack or picnic lunch box due to its portability and is a representative menu loved in Korean street snack culture, as children can easily enjoy it.

Sotteoksotteok is a Korean street food where sausages and tteok are alternately skewered on a long skewer, then coated with a sweet and spicy sauce and eaten. It is a simple and hearty snack that can be easily enjoyed at festivals or events.

Butter ojingeogui is a dish where squid is grilled in butter to enhance its rich and savory flavor. Its chewy texture and mild taste pair well with beer or as an appetizer, making it popular as a menu for simple outdoor parties or home parties.

음식 소개

꼬마김밥은 일반 김밥보다 훨씬 작게 만들어 한입에 쏙 들어가는 간편한 음식이다. 주로 단무지, 우엉, 당근, 계란지단 등 기본 재료로 간단히 만들 수 있으며, 매콤한 어묵볶음이나 참치마요 등 속재료에 변화를 주어 다양한 맛을 낸다. 휴대성이 좋아 간식이나 소풍 도시락으로 인기가 있으며, 아이들도 쉽게 즐길 수 있어 한국 길거리 분식 문화에서 사랑받는 대표 메뉴다.

소떡소떡은 길쭉한 꼬치에 소시지와 떡을 번갈아 꽂은 뒤, 달콤매콤한 소스를 발라 먹는 한국 길거리 음식이다. 간단하고 든든한 간식으로 축제나 행사장에서 쉽게 즐길 수 있다.

버터오징어구이는 오징어를 버터에 구워 고소하고 진한 풍미를 살린 음식이다. 쫄깃한 식감과 담백한 맛이 술안주로 어울려 간단한 야외파티나 홈파티 메뉴로 인기가 높다.

Cook 01

Kkomagimbap

꼬마김밥

Allergen Information: Eggs, Wheat

Spiciness Level: Mild

Way to Cook: Boiling, Pan-frying

RECIPE

 Ingredients(for 4 Servings)

Rice : 300g	밥 300g
Seaweed for Gimbap : 3 sheets	김밥용김 3장
Pickled Radish : 30g	단무지 30g
Spinach : 30g	시금치 30g
Carrot : 30g	당근 30g
Sesame Seeds : 5g	깨 5g
Sesame Oil : 15ml	참기름 15ml
Salt : 1g	소금 1g
Cooking Oil : 30ml	식용유 30ml
Water(for blanching) : 200ml	물(데치는 용도) 200ml

재료(4인분)

 Tip

- Kkomagimbap can have various flavors depending on the fillings. For a spicy kick, try adding chopped Cheongyang chili peppers. Adding bulgogi or cheese also creates a fantastic combination!

- 꼬마김밥은 속재료에 따라서 맛이 다르다. 매콤한 맛을 좋아하면 청양고추를 다져 넣어 땡초김밥을 만들자. 불고기나 치즈를 넣어도 환상의 조합!

PREPARATION

1 Thinly slice the carrots and pickled radish into 0.5cm strips.

당근과 단무지를 0.5cm 두께로 얇게 채썰어준다.

2 Cut the spinach into 10cm lengths.

시금치를 10cm 길이로 잘라준다.

COOKING STEPS

1 Add cooking oil to a preheated pan and stir-fry the sliced carrots with a pinch of salt.

식용유를 두르고 예열한 팬에 채썬 당근과 소금을 약간 넣고 볶는다.

2 Blanch the spinach briefly in boiling water with a little salt, then cool and remove excess moisture.

끓는 물에 소금을 한꼬집 넣은 후 시금치를 데친다. 데친 시금치를 식혀서 물기를 제거한다.

③ Mix the rice with salt, sesame seeds, and sesame oil thoroughly.

밥에 소금, 깨, 참기름을 넣고 잘 비벼준다.

④ Fold the seaweed once horizontally and once vertically to divide it into four parts.

김을 가로 세로로 한 번씩 접어 4등분한다.

5 Place the ingredients on the cut seaweed, roll it up, and lightly moisten the end with water to secure it.

자른 김 위에 재료들을 넣고 말다가, 끝에 물을 살짝 묻혀서 고정시킨다.

6 Brush with sesame oil and sprinkle sesame seeds.

참기름을 바른 후 깨를 뿌린다.

Cook 02

Sotteoksotteok

소떡소떡

Allergen Information

Wheat, Pork

알러지 정보 밀, 돼지고기

Spiciness Level

Mild

맵기 단계 순한맛

Way to Cook

Pan frying

조리 기법 팬 프라잉

RECIPE

Ingredients(for 4 Servings)
Tteok(for Tteokbokki) : 12 pieces
Vienna Sausages : 12 pieces
Cooking Oil : 30ml
Water(for blanching) : 500ml

재료(4인분)
떡(떡볶이용) 12개
비엔나 12개
식용유 30ml
물(데치는 용도) 500ml

Sauce
Ketchup : 4 tbsps
Gochujang : 2 tbsps
Soy Sauce : 1 tbsp
Minced Garlic : 1 tbsp
Corn Syrup : 4 tbsps
Parsley

소스
케첩 4큰술
고추장 2큰술
간장 1큰술
다진 마늘 1큰술
물엿 4큰술
파슬리

Tool
Wooden Skewers

도구
나무 꼬치

Tip
- Instead of gochujang sauce, you can also serve it with teriyaki, honey mustard, or garlic dipping sauce
- 고추장소스 대신 데리야끼, 허니머스터드, 갈릭디핑소스 등을 곁들여도 좋다.

PREPARATION

1 After blanching the tteok in boiling water for about 1 minute, cool them with cold water.

떡을 끓는 물에 1분간 데친 후 찬 물로 식혀준다.

2 Blanch the Vienna sausages for about 2 minutes, remove them from the water.

비엔나를 2분간 데친 후 건져준다.

COOKING STEPS

1 Skewer three pieces of Vienna sausage and three pieces of tteok alternately on each wooden skewer.

나무꼬치에 비엔나, 떡을 번갈아가며 각 3개씩 꽂는다.

2 Add oil to a pan and cook the skewers over low heat.

팬에 기름을 두른 후 약불에 굽는다.

③ Combine all the sauce ingredients in the pan and simmer over medium heat, stirring occasionally. Once it starts to bubble, turn off the heat.

소스 재료들을 모두 팬에 넣고 중불에 저어가며 끓이다 보글보글 할 때 불을 꺼준다.

④ Brush the sauce onto the skewers using a basting brush, then plate them in a dish and sprinkle with parsley for garnish.

붓으로 꼬치에 소스를 바르고, 그릇에 담고 파슬리를 뿌려 플레이팅한다.

RECIPE

 Ingredients(for 4 Servings)
Semi-dried Squid : 4
Butter : 150g

 Sauce
Mayonnaise : 3 tbsps
Lemon Juice : 1 tbsp
Sugar : 1 tbsp
Minced Garlic : 0.3 tsp
Soy Sauce : 0.5 tbsp
Cheongyang Chili Pepper : 1g
Sugar : 2g
Pepper : 0.5g
Salt : 0.1g

재료(4인분)
반건조 오징어 4마리
버터 150g

소스
마요네즈 3큰술
레몬즙 1큰술
설탕 1큰술
다진 마늘 0.3큰슬
간장 0.5큰술
청양고추 1g
설탕 2g
후추 0.5g
소금 0.1g

 Tip
- It tastes great even when made with jinmichae(dried squid) Instead of semi-dried squid.
- A potato masher is better than a spatula for pressing the squid.

- 반건조 오징어 대신 진미채로 만들어도 맛있다.
- 오징어를 눌러주는 데는 주걱보다 포테이토 매셔가 더 좋다.

PREPARATION

1 After removing the moisture from the semi-dried squid, cut both sides with scissors.

반건조 오징어의 물기를 제거한 후 양면을 가위로 잘라준다.

2 Combine all the sauce ingredients and mix well.

소스 재료를 모두 넣고 잘 섞어준다.

COOKING STEPS

1 Preheat the pan and melt the butter.

팬을 예열한 후 버터를 녹인다.

2 Add the prepared squid, season with salt and pepper, and cook, pressing gently with a spatula to prevent it from curling up.

손질된 오징어를 넣고 소금, 후추를 뿌린 후 말리지 않게 주걱으로 눌러주면서 굽는다.

3 Once the squid is fully cooked, place it on a plate, sprinkle with parsley, and set the sauce to accompany it in a sauce dish.

구운 오징어를 접시에 놓고 파슬리를 뿌린 후 같이 곁들여서 먹을 소스를 소스 그릇에 담는다.

Episode 04

Samgyetang

Date	Jul 15, 2024
Introduction	The summer of 2024 was especially hot! To mark the start of the hottest season, I prepared a nutritious meal for the T1 family.
Allergen Information	🐔 Chicken
Spiciness Level	🌶 Mild
Way to Cook	🍲 Boiling

일자	2024. 7. 15
소개	2024년 여름은 유난히 덥더라! 초복 맞이해 T1 가족을 위해 보양식을 준비했다.
알러지 정보	닭
맵기 단계	순한맛
조리 기법	끓이기

Shout out to Gumayusi at Chobok

삼계탕 – 초복에 구마유시 샤라웃

STORY

"What is the most beloved health food in Korea?" It's the food that everyone, regardless of age or gender, enjoys: samgyetang. The players' mealtimes are a bit different from the average person's. The last dinner is served at the time when others eat late-night snacks. Since they practice late into the night, it seems that late-night snacks aren't enough. They are at an age where hunger can't be ignored! Maybe that's why the cafeteria is filled with empty boxes of fried chicken the next day when I go to work. When we serve various flavors of fried chicken as a dinner menu, they're consumed in no time, with everyone loving it. While that always brings a smile to my face, I also worry about their health. So, I make sure to include healthier chicken dishes in their diet regularly, instead of fried foods.

우리나라에서 가장 사랑받는 보양식 1위는 무엇일까? 남녀노소 모두가 즐기는 그 음식, 바로 삼계탕이다. 선수들의 삼시세끼 식사시간은 좀 다르다. 마지막 저녁 식사가 남들이 야식을 먹는 시각에 제공된다. 야밤에도 연습을 하기 때문에 야식만으로 충분하지 않은 듯하다. 뒤돌아 서면 한창 배고플 나이가 아닌가! 그래서인지 다음날 출근하면 카페테리아에 치킨박스가 쌓여 있다. 간혹 저녁 메뉴로 다양한 맛의 치킨을 제공하면 가히 폭발적인 인기로 모든 메뉴가 순삭된다. 그때마다 기분이 좋아지지만, 한편으로 건강이 신경 쓰인다. 그래서 튀김 대신 건강한 닭요리를 주기적으로 식단에 포함시키고 있다.

Samgyetang is a staple menu item every summer. When I first introduced it, I was worried that there would be too much leftover, so I only served chicken legs in the soup. But to my surprise, it became so popular that I introduced bangyetang (a soup made with half a chicken). Was that the end? Not quite. The summer of 2024 was unusually hot, and people kept coming back for more. Eventually, I decided to serve full chicken portions—carefully prepared to ensure the chicken stayed intact. Given the large quantities required, I had to use a large pot, and with the chickens stacked on top of each other, making them prone to breaking apart.

Fortunately, the chickens turned out beautifully cooked,

Lee 'Gumayusi' Min-hyeong
'구마유시' 이민형 선수

and I couldn't help but smile a proud smile. It seemed like everyone was satisfied. Among them, player Lee Min-hyeong (Gumayushi) posted a thank you message on his Instagram story, tagging T1's official account: "Fans, be sure to enjoy Samgyetang!"

I was grateful that he enjoyed the meal and for his kind gesture of sharing T1's meal with his followers. To honor his thoughtful action, I'm sharing the samgyetang recipe with everyone.

📩 About the Dish

Samgyetang is a traditional summer dish made by slow-boiling a whole chicken stuffed with ginseng, jujube, garlic, and other ingredients. It's known for helping restore energy and vitality during the hot summer months, with a rich, flavorful broth and tender chicken. It's often enjoyed with a sprinkle of salt and pepper or with noodles, like a noodle soup. With its savory and mild flavor, Samgyetang is a beloved Korean health dish enjoyed year-round.

삼계탕은 여름 단골 메뉴다. 처음 선보일 때는 양이 많아 남을까 걱정해 닭다리만 제공했다. 웬걸! 그래서 반계탕을 선보였다.

반계탕이 끝일까? 2024년 초복은 유난히도 더웠다. 반계탕 받고 반계탕 더! 온전한 한 마리를 날개나 다리가 떨어지지 않도록 정성스럽게 삶았다. 워낙 양이 많다 보니 끓이는 통도 커야 했고 닭들이 겹쳐 있어서 부서지기 십상이었다.

다행히 이쁘게 삶아진 닭들을 보아하니 절로 아빠 미소가 지어졌다. 모든 식구가 만족하는 듯 보였다. 그중에 구마유시 이민형 선수가 삼계탕을 먹고 고맙게도 본인 인스타 스토리에 티밥 인스타를 태그해줬다. "팬 여러분~ 다들 삼계탕 드세요." 맛있게 먹어 줘서도 고마웠고, 이렇게 팬분들에게 티밥을 소개해줘서 고마웠다. 티밥을 팬들에게 소개한 구마유시 선수의 센스를 칭송하며, 그리고 감사해하며 삼계탕 레시피를 공개한다.

음식 소개

삼계탕은 여름철 대표 보양식으로 닭 안에 인삼, 대추, 마늘 등을 넣고 푹 끓여 만든 음식이다. 더위에 지친 원기를 회복하는 데 도움을 주며, 국물이 깊고 닭고기가 부드럽다. 먹을 때 소금, 후추를 곁들이거나 면을 넣어 국수처럼 즐기기도 한다. 고소하고 담백한 맛으로 계절을 불문하고 사랑받는 한국 전통 보양식이다.

RECIPE

Ingredients
Chicken : 1 whole(young chicken, 500g)
Glutinous Rice : 1 cup
Garlic : 6 cloves, whole
Ginseng : 5cm
Jujube : 3 pieces(dried)
Ginger : 2.5cm
Onion : 1, quartered
Green Onion : 2
Salt and Pepper

재료
닭 한 마리(어린 닭, 약 500g)
찹쌀 1컵
마늘 6쪽, 통째로
인삼(약 5cm)
대추 3개(말린 것)
생강 한 조각(약 2.5cm)
양파 1개, 4등분
대파 2대
소금과 후추

Broth
Water : 12 cups
Korean Soy Sauce : 2 tbsps
Sesame Oil : 1 tbsp
Salt(adjust to taste) : 1 tsp
Black Pepper : 1 tsp

육수
물 12컵
간장 2큰술(한국 간장)
참기름 1큰술
소금 1작은술(기호에 맞게)
후추 1작은술

Optional Garnish
Chopped Green Onion
Thinly Sliced Cheongyang Chili Pepper
A Drop of Sesame Oil

선택적 고명
다진 대파
얇게 썬 청양고추
참기름 한 방울

Tool
Ttukbaegi(Stone Pot)

도구
뚝배기

Tip
- You can boil the leftover glutinous rice and broth to make a nutritious chicken porridge—two birds with one stone.
- Adding mala sauce turns it into a spicy, flavorful mala samgyetang.
- For an upgraded version, add scorched rice, abalone, or herbal ingredients while boiling to enhance both the nutrition and flavor.

- 닭살을 먹고 남긴 찹쌀과 국물을 끓여서 닭죽을 해 먹으면 일석이조.
- 마라소스를 넣으면 마라 삼계탕이 된다.
- 끓일 때 누룽지, 전복, 한방 약재 등을 넣으면 영양 만점, 맛은 업그레이드.

PREPARATION

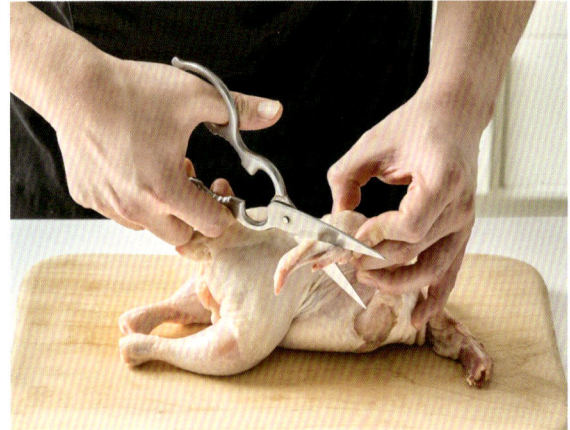

1. Soak the glutinous rice in water for about 1 hour in advance.

   찹쌀을 1시간 정도 물에 미리 불린다.

2. Wash the chicken thoroughly and trim the fatty areas around the tail, neck, and wing tips.

   닭을 잘 씻어서 기름이 많은 꼬리와 목, 양날개 끝을 손질한다.

3. Make holes on both sides inside the thighs.

   허벅지 안쪽으로 좌우에 구멍을 낸다.

COOKING STEPS

1 Stuff the chicken with the prepared ginseng, glutinous rice, garlic, and jujubes.

준비한 인삼, 찹쌀, 마늘, 대추를 닭 속에 넣는다.

2 Add an appropriate amount of soaked glutinous rice to the chicken.

불려놓은 찹쌀을 닭에 적당량 넣는다.

3 Insert cotton thread into both holes on the legs and tie the legs together.

다리 양쪽 구멍에 무명실을 넣어 양 다리를 묶어준다.

4 Place the chicken in a pot filled with water, ensuring that the chicken is submerged with its belly facing up.

물을 채운 냄비에 닭의 배가 올라오도록 넣는다.

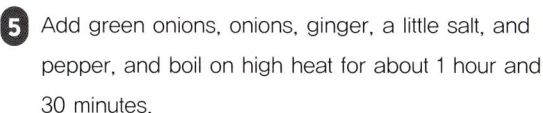

5. Add green onions, onions, ginger, a little salt, and pepper, and boil on high heat for about 1 hour and 30 minutes.

   파, 양파, 생강, 약간의 소금, 후추를 넣고 센 불에 1시간 30분가량 끓인다.

6. Add sesame oil, soy sauce, and pepper.

   참기름, 간장, 후추를 넣는다.

7. Carefully place it into a ttukbaegi(stone pot).

   뚝배기에 정성스럽게 담는다.

Episode 05

Welcoming 'Gatnaon Matdori'

빠에야 & 립 바베큐
– '갓 나온 맛도리'를 환영합니다

Paella & Rib Barbecue

Date   Jun 5, 2024

Introduction   The YouTube channel SBS News 'Gatnaon Matdori' paid a visit to T1! Here, we introduce the paella and BBQ ribs that were showcased during that visit.

일자   2024. 6. 5.

소개   유튜브 채널 스브스뉴스 '갓 나온 맛도리'가 T1에 출동했다! 그때 소개한 빠에야와 립 바베큐를 소개한다.

STORY

The SBS YouTube channel 'Gatnaon Matdori' is visiting. 'Gatnaon Matdori' is a program where the producer personally explores and visits popular eateries. It is renowned for its detailed explanations of flavors and vivid introductions. Coincidentally, on that very day, they decided to visit the cafeteria of a large entertainment company first. While I was excited, the pressure was immense. Selecting the menu was the top priority.

After much deliberation, I decided to return to the roots of my culinary journey: paella, a traditional Spanish home-cooked dish. Seventeen years ago, this dish was unfamiliar, but it has now become a much-loved menu item. Back then, it was so novel that most people would ask, "Isn't this curry rice?"

SBS 유튜브 채널 '갓나온 맛도리'가 방문한다. '갓나온 맛도리'는 PD가 직접 발로 뛰며 맛집을 탐방하는 프로그램이다. 맛에 대한 섬세한 설명과 생생한 소개로 유명하다. 하필이면 당일, 대형 엔터테인먼트 회사의 구내식당을 먼저 방문한다니, 기대되는 한편으로 부담감이 이만저만이 아니었다. 메뉴 선정이 우선이었다.

고민 끝에 내 요리 인생의 원점으로 돌아가보았다. 빠에야, 스페인 가정식 요리. 17년 전만 해도 생소했던 이 요리는 이제는 많은 사랑을 받는 메뉴가 되었다. 당시만 해도 십중팔구는 "카레밥 아니에요?"라고 물을 정도로 낯선 음식이었다.

To. 선수들
뭐니 뭐니 해도 건강이 최고

By chance, I became captivated by the allure of paella and devoted myself to mastering it. It must have taken several batches of rice. When preparing the broth, the balance of chicken, pork, and seafood, the heat level, the simmering time, and the frequency with which the lid is opened—all of these factors play a crucial role in shaping the flavor. How captivating this dish is!

우연한 계기로 빠에야의 매력에 흠뻑 빠져 연구에 매진했다. 쌀 몇 가마를 희생시켰을 터. 육수를 만들 때 닭, 돼지, 해물 조합과 비율, 불의 세기, 뜸 들이는 시간, 뚜껑 열고 닫기에 따라 맛이 천차만별이다. 얼마나 매력적인 요리인가!

I decided to feature paella alongside barbecue ribs to provide sufficient protein. The sweltering weather in early June was quite challenging, but since the program is all about vividly showcasing flavors, I couldn't give up on grilling barbecue ribs over charcoal on the rooftop. So during the interview with the producer, I was grilling the ribs over charcoal. Tears and a runny nose were inevitable—I had to grill the meat and conduct the interview simultaneously regardless. It was utterly chaotic. During the interview, I brought up spinach and carrot juice. Both are rich in vitamin A and great for boosting immunity, so I serve them occasionally to our players and staff who spend long hours in front of screens.

빠에야와 단백질을 채워줄 바베큐립으로 메뉴를 정했다. 6월 초의 무더운 날씨는 그리 만만치 않았지만, 생생하게 맛을 소개하는 프로그램인 만큼 옥상에서 숯불 BBQ로 직접 구운 바베큐립을 포기할 수 없었다. 지금에서야 말하지만 인터뷰 중에 숯불로 립을 굽고 있었다. 눈물, 콧물은 나지, 고기는 구워야지, 인터뷰는 해야지. 정신이 하나도 없었다.
인터뷰 중에 시금치와 당근을 섞은 주스까지 말해버렸다. 이 두 재료는 비타민 A가 풍부해 면역력 강화에 좋다.

Since some people aren't fond of carrots, I also add them to the meat seasoning to ensure they get a natural intake. This way, they benefit from not only protein but also essential minerals and vitamins—a double advantage. But this was a secret... I accidentally let it slip!

그래서 모니터를 오래 보는 우리 선수단과 직원들에게 틈틈이 제공하고 있다. 당근을 싫어할 수 있어, 주스가 아니더라도 고기 양념에 넣어 자연스러운 섭취를 꾀하고 있다. 이렇게 하면 단백질은 물론 무기질과 비타민까지 일석이조로 섭취할 수 있으니 말이다. 그런데 이건 비밀인데... 말해버렸다!

About the Dish
Paella is Spain's iconic rice dish, originally from the Valencia region. It's made by cooking rice in a wide pan, spread thinly, with seafood, chicken, and vegetables, and coloring the rice yellow with saffron. The slightly crispy rice at the bottom, known as "socarrat," is considered a delicacy. Renowned worldwide for its rich flavors and enticing aromas, paella stands out as a beloved traditional dish, thanks to the perfect harmony of its ingredients.

음식 소개
빠에야는 스페인 대표 쌀요리로, 주로 발렌시아 지역에서 유래했다. 해산물, 닭고기, 채소 등을 올리며 샤프란으로 노란빛을 낸 밥을 넓은 팬에 얇게 펼쳐 조리하는 것이 특징이다. 바닥에 살짝 눌어붙은 밥인 '소카라트'가 별미로 꼽히며, 여러 재료가 어우러진 풍부한 맛과 향으로 전 세계적으로 사랑받고 있다.

Cook 01

Paella

빠에야

Allergen Information	Spiciness Level	Way to Cook
 Squid Shrimp	 Mild	 Braising
알러지 정보 오징어, 새우	맵기 단계 순한맛	조리 기법 볶음찜

RECIPE

Ingredients
Soaked Rice : 200g
Shrimp : 8
Mussels : 10
Squid Body : 1
Onion : 1
Green Bell Pepper : 1
Red Bell Pepper : 1
Cherry Tomato : 8

재료
불린 쌀 200g
새우 8마리
홍합 10개
오징어 몸통 1마리
양파 1개
청피망 1개
홍피망 1개
방울토마토 8개

Broth
Chicken Stock : 30g
Water (Mussel Broth) : 300ml
Olive Oil : 150ml
Lemon : 0.5
Parsley : 20g
Paella Seasoning : 12g
Minced Garlic : 50g

육수
치킨스톡 30g
물(홍합육수) 300ml
올리브오일 150ml
레몬 0.5개
파슬리 20g
빠에야시즈닝 12g
다진 마늘 50g

Tip
- Serving it over tomato purée sauce gives it an omurice-like taste.
- It also tastes good when using meat (chicken, pork, beef) instead of seafood.
- Adding more broth and finishing with cheese makes an excellent risotto paella.
- If the seasoning is insufficient, adjust the taste with salt and pepper.

- 토마토 퓨레 소스에 얹어 먹으면 오므라이스 맛이 난다.
- 해산물 대신 육류(닭, 돼지, 소고기)를 활용해도 맛있다.
- 육수를 더 넣어서 치즈로 마무리하면 훌륭한 리소또 빠에야가 된다.
- 간이 부족하면 소금, 후추로 간을 입맛에 맞추자.

PREPARATION

① Soak the rice for 30 minutes.

쌀을 30분간 불린다.

② Cut the onion and bell pepper into 2 x 2cm pieces.

양파, 피망을 2 x 2cm 크기로 자른다.

③ Cut the lemon and cherry tomatoes in half.

레몬과 방울토마토를 반으로 자른다.

④ Slice the squid into 1cm thick pieces.

오징어를 1cm 두께로 썰어준다.

COOKING STEPS

1 Add enough water to cover the mussels and boil for about 10 minutes. Once boiled, remove the mussels and set aside the broth.

홍합이 잠길 정도로 물을 넣고 10분간 끓인다. 다 끓으면 홍합을 건져내 육수를 따로 보관한다.

2 Saute the onion, bell pepper, and cherry tomatoes in a pan with olive oil.

올리브오일을 두룬 팬에 양파, 피망, 방울토마토를 볶아둔다.

3 Saute the shrimp in a pan with olive oil, cooking them on both sides until well done.

올리브오일을 두른 팬에 새우를 앞뒤로 잘 구워둔다.

4 Heat olive oil in a wide pan, then sauté garlic and soaked rice.

넓은 팬에 올리브오일을 두르고 마늘과 불린 쌀을 넣고 볶아준다.

5 When the rice becomes translucent, add paella seasoning and squid, and saute.

쌀이 투명해지면 빠에야 시즈닝과 오징어를 넣고 볶는다.

6 Mix chicken stock into the mussel broth, then pour it into the pan.

홍합 육수에 치킨스톡을 넣어 섞은 후 팬에 붓는다.

7 Add the previously sauteed vegetables, shrimp, and blanched mussels.

미리 볶아둔 야채와 새우, 데친 홍합을 넣는다.

8 Simmer over medium heat for 15 minutes, then let it rest for about 10 minutes. Garnish with parsley and plate.

15분간 중불로 졸인 후 10분간 뜸을 들여 완성한다. 파슬리를 뿌려 플레이팅한다.

Cook 02

Rib Barbecue
립 바베큐

Allergen Information	Spiciness Level	Way to Cook
 Pork	 Mild	 Roasting
알러지 정보 돼지고기	맵기 단계 순한맛	조리 기법 굽기

RECIPE

 Ingredients (for 2 Servings)
Pork Ribs : 1kg
Radish : 200g
Green Onion : 2
Whole Black Peppercorns : 10
Bay Leaves : 3
Rosemary : 1 sprig
Water : 3000ml

재료(2인분)
등갈비 1kg
무 200g
대파잎 2장
통후추 10알
월계수 3장
로즈마리 1줄기
물 3000ml

 Broth
Barbecue Sauce : 3 tbsps
Corn Syrup : 1 tbsp
Soy Sauce : 1 tbsp
Tomato Ketchup : 1 tbsp
Minced Garlic : 1 tsp

육수
바베큐소스 3큰술
물엿 1큰술
간장 1큰술
토마토케첩 1큰술
다진 마늘 1작은술

 Tip
- If you simmer the sauce over low heat until it thickens, it transforms into a dipping sauce.
- Brushing the sauce on the meat one or two more times while grilling helps the seasoning penetrate better.
- You can also bake it in an air fryer instead of an oven.

- 소스를 약한 불에서 뭉근히 끓여서 걸쭉하게 만들면 찍먹 소스로 변신한다.
- 소스를 한두 번 더 발라서 구우면 간이 더 잘 밴다.
- 오븐 대신 에어프라이어에 구워도 된다.

PREPARATION

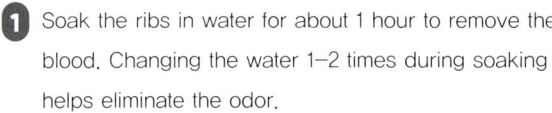

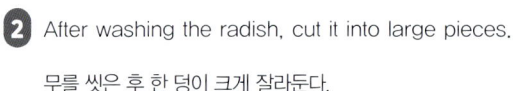

1 Soak the ribs in water for about 1 hour to remove the blood. Changing the water 1-2 times during soaking helps eliminate the odor.

등갈비를 물에 1시간 정도 담가 핏물을 뺀다. 중간에 1~2번 물을 갈아 핏물을 빼주면 냄새 제거에 더 좋다.

2 After washing the radish, cut it into large pieces.

무를 씻은 후 한 덩이 크게 잘라둔다.

3 Wash 2 green onion stalks.

대파 2쪽을 씻어둔다.

4 Sauce Mix barbecue sauce, corn syrup, soy sauce, tomato ketchup, and minced garlic well.

소스 바베큐소스, 물엿, 간장, 토마토케첩, 다진 마늘을 잘 섞어준다.

COOKING STEPS

1 Place the ribs in enough water to submerge them, along with radish, green onion leaves, whole peppercorns, bay leaves, and rosemary, and bring to a boil. Once boiling, simmer the ribs over medium heat for about 40 minutes.

갈비가 잠길 정도 양의 물에 무, 대파잎, 통후추, 월계수잎, 로즈마리, 갈비를 넣어 끓인다. 물이 끓으면 40분간 중불에서 삶는다.

2 Bake the cooked ribs in a 200°C oven for about 5 minutes until golden brown.

익힌 갈비를 200도 오븐에 5분간 노릇하게 굽는다.

3 Apply the sauce to the grilled ribs.

구워진 갈비에 소스를 바른다.

4 Bake again in the oven for 5 minutes.

오븐에 5분간 다시 굽는다.

5 Serve on a plate.

접시에 담는다.

Date	Jul 20, 2022
Introduction	We are grateful for the passionate support from Vietnamese fans for TBap. To show our appreciation, we prepared Vietnamese dishes especially for our T1 Vietnamese fans.

일자	2022. 7. 20
소개	베트남 팬들이 티밥에 보내주신 뜨거운 관심에 감사를! 그래서 T1 베트남 팬을 위한 베트남 음식을 준비했다.

STORY

When the 'TBap' Instagram account reached its two-year anniversary, it had garnered a considerable amount of attention, which was quite encouraging. Curious to see who was visiting our page, I discovered that not only domestic fans but also a significant number of international fans were following us. Among them, Vietnamese fans constituted a large proportion.

I wanted to give something back to our Vietnamese fans. So, for a special treat, I decided to capture the essence of a "Vietnamese night market." Since it was summer, instead of serving pho, I chose the refreshing buncha. I was confident that adding banh mi would truly evoke the night market atmosphere.

"It's my first time trying banh mi, it's crazy!", "Can I have another one?" The reactions were as hot as the summer weather. "I prepared plenty, so feel free to enjoy as much as you want!"

인스타에 티밥 계정을 운영한 지 2년이 지났을 때다. 그간 적지 않은 관심을 받아 나름 고무된 기분에, 어떤 분들이 많이 찾아주시는지 살펴보았다. 국내 팬뿐만 아니라 해외 팬도 적지 않았다. 그중에서 베트남 팬 비중이 높았다.

베트남 팬에게 무언가 선물을 주고 싶었다. 그래서 특식으로 '베트남 야시장' 느낌을 살려보기로 했다. 여름이니까 쌀국수 대신, 시원한 분짜를 선택했다. 거기에 반미까지 곁들이면 야시장 느낌이 확실히 살 거라는 확신이 섰다.

"반미 처음 먹어 보는데 미쳤어요!", "하나 더 먹어도 되나요?" 여름 날씨처럼 뜨거운 반응이 이어졌다. "넉넉히 준비했으니 마음껏 드세요!"

In my personal opinion, buncha is a dish that people in Korea, who are accustomed to cold noodles, would enjoy. Not only is the taste great, but the combination of carbohydrates and protein is also excellent, making me feel like I should present it again before summer ends.

Above all, hearing affectionate and slightly exaggerated comments like "It's even more delicious than what I had in Vietnam!" gave me an immense boost of energy. I hope it became a pleasant memory for our Vietnamese fans who love the TBap account!

🍽 About the Dish

Buncha is a representative noodle dish from Hanoi, Vietnam, consisting of charcoal-grilled pork, thin rice noodles, and aromatic herbs, served with a tangy and sweet nuoc mam sauce. The fresh and mild flavors harmonize beautifully, making it a quintessential delicacy that captures the essence of local street food culture.

Banh mi is a Vietnamese-style baguette sandwich, featuring a crispy baguette filled with meat, cucumber, pickled carrots, cilantro, and more, enhancing its rich flavors. It is the result of blending the bread culture from the French colonial era with local Vietnamese ingredients, making it light and easy to enjoy, loved worldwide.

개인적인 생각으로 분짜는 냉면에 익숙한 우리나라 사람들이 은근히 좋아할 만한 음식이다. 맛도 맛이지만 탄수화물과 단백질 조합이 좋아 여름이 다 가기 전에 다시 선보여야겠다 생각이 들 정도다. 무엇보다 "베트남에서 먹은 맛보다 더 맛있어요!"라는 애정과 과장을 섞은 칭찬을 들으니 에너지가 무한 충전되는 기분이 들었다. 티밥 계정을 사랑해주신 베트남 팬들께 즐거운 추억이 되었길!

음식 소개

분짜는 베트남 하노이를 대표하는 면요리로, 숯불에 구운 돼지고기와 얇은 쌀국수, 향긋한 허브를 새콤달콤한 느억맘소스에 곁들여 먹는다. 상큼하고 담백한 맛이 조화를 이루며, 현지 길거리 음식문화의 정취를 느낄 수 있는 대표적인 별미다.

반미는 베트남식 바게트 샌드위치로, 바삭한 바게트 속에 고기, 오이, 당근 절임, 고수 등을 넣어 풍미를 살린다. 프랑스 식민시대의 빵 문화와 베트남 현지 재료가 결합한 결과물로, 가볍고 간편하게 즐길 수 있어 세계적으로 사랑받는다.

Cook 01

Buncha

분짜

Allergen Information

Pork

알러지 정보 돼지고기

Spiciness Level

Mild

맵기 단계 순한맛

Way to Cook

Sauteing

조리 기법 볶기

RECIPE

 Ingredients(for 2 Servings)

Rice Vermicelli(1mm) : 125g
Lettuce : 80g
Red Beet : 80g
Radicchio : 80g
Cilantro : 10g
Bean Sprouts : 100g

 재료(2인분)

쌀국수(1mm) 125g
양상추 80g
레드비트 80g
라디치오 80g
고수 10g
숙주 100g

 Seasoning

Pork Shoulder : 300g
Soy Sauce : 3 tbsps
Minced Garlic : 1 tsp
Cooking Wine : 2 tbsps
Oligo Syrup : 1.5 tbsps
Sesame Oil : 1 tsp
Ginger : 1 tsp
Pepper : a little
Cooking Oil : 30ml

양념

돼지 앞다리살 300g
간장 3큰술
다진 마늘 1작은술
맛술 2큰술
올리고당 1.5큰술
참기름 1작은술
생강 1작은술
후추 약간
식용유 30ml

 Sugar Water

Water : 200ml
Sugar : 350g

설탕물

물 200ml
설탕 350g

 Buncha Sauce

Sugar Water : 13 tbsps
Hot Water : 5 tbsps
Fish Sauce : 6 tbsps
Lemon Juice : 2 tbsps
Minced Garlic : 1 tbsp
Red Chili Pepper : 2g

분짜소스

설탕물	13큰술
뜨거운 물	5큰술
피시소스	6큰술
레몬즙	2큰술
다진 마늘	1큰술
홍고추	2g

Tip

- Adding ice to the sauce makes it cool and delicious.

- 소스에 얼음을 넣으면 시원하고 맛있게 먹을 수 있다.

PREPARATION

1 Soak the rice noodles in cold water for about 30 minutes.

쌀국수를 찬 물에 30분간 불린다.

2 Mix soy sauce, minced garlic, cooking wine, oligo syrup, sesame oil, ginger, and black pepper to create the meat seasoning sauce.

간장, 다진 마늘, 맛술, 올리고당, 참기름, 생강, 후추를 섞어 고기 양념 소스를 만든다.

3 Slice radicchio and lettuce into 0.1cm thick pieces, and cut chicory into 4cm long sections.

라디치오와 양상추를 0.1cm 두께로, 치커리를 4cm 두께로 썬다.

4 <u>Buncha Sauce</u> Slice red chili peppers to 0.1cm thickness.

<u>소스</u> 홍고추를 0.1cm 두께로 썬다.

5 Mix sugar water, hot water, fish sauce, lemon juice, minced garlic, and red chili peppers well.

설탕물, 뜨거운 물, 피시소스, 레몬즙, 다진 마늘, 홍고추를 잘 섞어준다.

COOKING STEPS

1 Marinate the meat with the seasoning for 30 minutes.

고기에 양념을 섞은 후 30분간 숙성시켜준다.

2 Briefly blanch the bean sprouts and noodles in water for about 30 seconds, then rinse with cold water and drain well.

숙주와 면은 30초 정도 물에 살짝만 데치고, 찬 물에 씻은 후 물기를 빼준다.

3 Preheat the pan, coat with cooking oil, and carefully stir-fry the marinated meat until golden brown, being careful not to burn it.

팬을 예열 후 식용유를 두르고, 숙성시켜둔 고기를 타지 않게 잘 저어가며 노릇하게 굽는다.

4 Serve the rice noodles and meat in a bowl, accompanied by a chilled sauce with ice.

쌀국수와 고기를 그릇에 담고, 얼음을 넣은 시원한 소스와 먹는다.

Cook 02

Banh Mi

반미

Allergen Information	Spiciness Level	Way to Cook
 Wheat Pork	 Mild	 Sauteing
알러지 정보 돼지고기	맵기 단계 순한맛	조리 기법 볶기

RECIPE

 Ingredients(for 2 Servings)
Banh Mi Baguette(78g) : 2
Cilantro : 30g
Jalapeño : 15g

재료(2인분)
반미바게트(78g) 2개
고수 30g
할라피뇨 15g

 Marinade for Meat
Pork Shoulder : 300g
Sugar : 3 tbsps
Soy Sauce : 3 tbsps
Oyster Sauce : 1 tbsp
Oligo Syrup : 1 tbsp
Minced Garlic : 1 tsp
Ground Ginger : 0.5 tsp
Pepper : 0.5 tsp

고기 양념
돼지 앞다리살 300g
설탕 3큰술
간장 3큰술
굴소스 1큰술
올리고당 1큰술
다진 마늘 1작은술
생강가루 0.5작은술
후추 0.5작은술

 Pickled Onions
Onion : 300g
Sugar : 3 tbsps
Vinegar : 3 tbsps
Salt : 1 tsp
Water : 1 cup

양파 절임
양파 300g
설탕 3큰술
식초 3큰술
소금 1작은술
물 1컵

 Sandwich Sauce
Sriracha : 1 tbsp
Mayonnaise : 2 tbsps
Sugar : 1 tbsp
Fish Sauce : 0.5 tbsp

샌드위치 소스
스리라차 1큰술
마요네즈 2큰술
설탕 1큰술
피시소스 0.5큰술

 Tip

- If you prefer a soft texture over a crispy one, avoid heating the bread in the oven!
- Replacing the meat with shrimp or scrambled eggs creates a light and diet-friendly dish – great!
- When baking bread without an oven, you can toast it on a preheated pan on low heat.

- 바삭한 느낌보다 부드러운 느낌을 즐긴다면 오븐에 굽지 말자!
- 고기를 새우나 스크램블로 대체하면 담백한 다이어트 식으로 굿!
- 오븐이 없을 땐 팬에서 약불로 빵을 구워도 된다.

PREPARATION

1 Slice the onions into thin strips approximately 0.1cm wide. Marinate them with sugar, vinegar, salt, and water for about 1 hour.

양파를 0.1cm 두께로 채썰어준다. 채썬 양파에 설탕, 식초, 소금, 물을 넣고 1시간 정도 절인다.

2 Mix Sriracha, mayonnaise, sugar, and fish sauce together to create the sandwich sauce.

스리라차, 마요네즈, 설탕, 피시소스를 잘 섞어 샌드위치 소스를 만든다.

3 Combine sugar, soy sauce, oyster sauce, oligo syrup, minced garlic, ginger powder, and black pepper to prepare the meat marinade.

설탕, 간장, 굴소스, 올리고당, 다진 마늘, 생강가루, 후추를 잘 섞어 고기 양념을 만든다.

COOKING STEPS

1 Heat the bread in an oven at 180°C for 5 minutes until golden brown.

빵을 오븐에서 180도로 5분간 노릇하게 굽는다.

2 Marinate the pork in seasoning sauce and let it sit for at least 30 minutes.

돼지고기를 양념장에 버무린 후 30분 이상 숙성시킨다.

3 Saute the marinated meat in a pan with cooking oil on high heat, then use a torch to add a smoky flavor.

예열된 팬에 식용유를 두른 후 숙성된 고기를 센 불로 볶는다. 토치로 그을려 훈연향을 첨가한다.

4 Cut the bread in half and spread Sriracha sauce on both sides.

빵을 반으로 가른 다음 스리라차소스를 양면에 바른다.

5. Spread sauce on one side, add pickled onions, then place the grilled meat, jalapeños, and cilantro on top.

한쪽 면에 소스를 바르고, 절인 양파를 올리고, 그위에 구운 고기, 할라피뇨, 고수를 올려준다.

6. Cover with the other half of the bread, and it's done!

빵을 덮으면 끝!

Episode 07

Date	May 18, 2023
Introduction	While watching Faker's personal stream, I discovered his top-tier menu. As soon as we met, I asked him about it. I wanted to make it just the way he liked.

일자	2023. 5. 18
소개	Faker 선수 개인방송을 보다 1티어 메뉴 발견. 마주치자마자 물었다. 원하는 맛, 그대로 만들어주고 싶어서.

Malatang & Jisamsun

"Aha! I see, Faker likes malatang!!"
I believe that a chef should have a sense of responsibility as if they're making food for their own family. That's why I always remind my colleagues about this. You might think it's an overstatement, especially in today's world, but for me, it's essential. Remember when you used to ask your mom, "Mom, can you make curry?" Didn't we all have those moments when we'd ask for food we craved? And every time, mom would make it. So when someone tells me they're craving something, I always try to provide it.
During my weekly shifts, I take the subway. For about an hour and a half, I scroll through social media, looking for trending foods or watching cooking videos from famous chefs to get meal ideas. One day, I watched Faker's stream, and he mentioned, "I'm really into malatang these days." The moment I heard that, I immediately placed an order for malatang from a popular spot. I wanted to deliver the best possible taste.

"아하! 페이커 선수는 마라탕을 좋아하는구나!!"
셰프는 내 가족이 먹는 음식을 만든다는 사명감이 있어야 한다고 생각한다. 그래서 함께 일하는 동료에게 늘 신신당부한다. 가족이라니, 요즘 같은 세상에 오버하는 거 아닌가라고 생각이 들지도 모르겠지만, 적어도 난 그래야 한다고 생각한다. 엄마 "나 카레 해줘" 누구나 먹고 싶은 음식을 엄마한테 주문하던 기억이 있지 않은가? 그때마다 엄마는 내 바람을 들어주셨다. 그래서 나도 누군가 뭐 먹고 싶다고 하면, 그 음식을 제공하는 편이다.

주간 근무를 할 때는 지하철을 이용한다. 약 1시간 반 동안 SNS에서 요즘 핫한 음식을 찾거나, 유명 셰프의 요리 영상을 보면서 식단 아이디어를 찾는다. 어느 날은 페이커 선수의 방송을 보게 되었다. "마라탕에 꽂혔습니다" 페이커 선수의 이 말을 듣고 나서 그날 바로 유명한 마라탕 음식점에서 포장 주문을 했다. 가능하면 최고의 맛을 제공하고 싶었기 때문이다.

Lee 'Faker' Sang-hyeok
'페이커' 이상혁 선수

When I tried it, I discovered it had a unique charm – spicy yet light, and incredibly appetizing. "Ah, so this is why everyone's talking about malatang these days", I thought to myself. Just then, Faker walked into the restaurant area, so I asked him if he'd be interested in having malatang as a meal option. "Don't you think some people might not like it?" he replied.

먹어보니 뭔가 얼큰하면서 담백하고 군침 흘리게 하는 그런 매력이 있었다. '아! 이래서 요즘 마라탕 마라탕하는구나' 혼자 생각을 했다. 때마침 페이커 선수가 식당에 들어왔길래 마라탕을 식사 메뉴로 내보면 어떨지 물어봤다. "다른 분들은 호불호가 있지 않을까요?"

Such a thoughtful response, always considering others! Confident that I could make it accessible for everyone, I told him I'd prepare it for next week's menu, to which he responded with excitement, saying he was looking forward to it.

Get ready for the recipe! A health-conscious version, with less spice and oil. It's time to reveal the secret recipe!

역시, 타인을 배려하는 멋진 대답! 누구나 먹을 수 있게 만들 자신이 있던 터라 다음 주 메뉴로 준비해보겠다 말했더니 기대하겠다고 화답해주었다.

기대하시라 건강을 생각해서 매운맛과 기름기를 덜어낸 레시피 개봉박두! 비밀 레시피를 이제부터 만나보자.

About the Dish

Malatang is a spicy and numbing hot pot dish from the Sichuan province of China, where a variety of ingredients are chosen and cooked in a spicy broth. The combination of pungent Sichuan spices and red chili oil creates a numbing and spicy taste, and the ability to customize the flavor by selecting different ingredients is a key part of its popularity.

Jisamsun (known as "Dìsānxiān" in Chinese, meaning "three fresh ingredients from the earth") is a home-style Chinese dish made by stir-frying eggplant, potatoes, and bell peppers in oil. The ingredients offer a tender and slightly sweet flavor, while the mild sauce adds a savory depth, making it a perfect accompaniment to rice.

음식 소개

마라탕은 중국 사천 지방의 얼얼하고 매운 국물 요리로, 각종 재료를 선택해 매운 국물에 끓여 먹는 방식이 특징이다. 알싸한 마라 향신료와 붉은 고추기름이 어우러져 맵고 얼얼한 맛을 즐길 수 있으며, 재료에 따라 무한히 변주 가능한 풍미가 인기 비결이다.

지삼선은 중국어 '디싼셴'으로 불리며 '땅에서 나는 세 가지 신선한 재료'라는 뜻이다. 가지, 감자, 피망을 기름에 볶아 만든 중국 가정식 요리다. 재료들이 부드럽고 달큰한 풍미를 내며, 담백한 소스가 감칠맛을 더해 밥반찬으로도 좋다.

Cook 01

Malatang

마라탕

Allergen Information

Shrimp   Pork

알러지 정보 새우, 돼지고기

Spiciness Level

Spicy

맵기 단계 시바까

Way to Cook

Simmering

조리 방법 부글부글 끓이기

RECIPE

 Ingredients(for 2 Servings)

Oyster Mushrooms : 100g	느타리버섯 100g
Wood Ear Mushrooms : 20g	목이버섯 20g
Tofu Skin : 50g	푸주 50g
Fish Balls : 50g	피시볼 50g
Vienna Sausage : 50g	비엔나 50g
Cilantro : 20g	고수 20g
Enoki Mushrooms : 20g	팽이버섯 20g
Bok Choy : 30g	청경채 30g
Udon Noodles : 200g	우동면 200g
Cooking Oil : 50ml	식용유 50ml

재료(2인분)

 Broth

Chili Oil : 5 tbsps	고추기름 5큰술
Doubanjiang : 1 tbsp	두반장 1큰술
Oyster Sauce : 2 tbsps	굴소스 2큰술
Liquid Maggi Sichuan Sauce : 1 tbsp	매기액상 쓰촨소스 1큰술
Water : 4 cups	물 4컵

육수

 Tools

Soup Bowl

도구

면기

 Tip

- Tofu skin takes about 3 hours to soak in cold water, but if you blanch it over medium-low heat, 10–15 minutes is enough.
- Adding beef bone broth to the soup will give it a rich and deep flavor.
- If you want to add meat, saute it first, drain any excess oil, and then add it. This way, you can enjoy a cleaner-tasting malatang.

- 푸주는 찬 물에 불리면 3시간 정도 걸리지만 중약불로 데치면 10~15분이면 충분하다.
- 국물에 사골육수를 넣으면 깊고 진한 마라탕을 느낄 수 있다.
- 고기를 넣고 싶다면, 볶은 후 기름을 살짝 빼고 넣자. 그러면 더 깔끔한 마라탕을 먹을 수 있다.

PREPARATION

1 Cut the bok choy into quarters, then slice each half.

청경채를 4등분하여 절반으로 자른다.

2 Tear the oyster mushrooms and enoki mushrooms into pieces.

느타리버섯과 팽이버섯을 잘 뜯어둔다.

COOKING STEPS

1 Boil the tofu skin on medium-low heat for 10-15 minutes, then remove it.

푸주를 중약불로 10~15분로 끓인 후, 건진다.

2 Add 5 tablespoons of chili oil to a pan, then add 1 tablespoon of doubanjiang and stir-fry.

팬에 고추기름 5큰술, 두반장 1큰술을 넣고 볶아준다.

3 When the doubanjiang starts to dissolve, add 2 tablespoons of oyster sauce and stir-fry on medium heat.

두반장이 풀어지면 굴소스 2큰술을 넣고 중불로 볶는다.

4 Pour in 4 cups of water, then add 1 tablespoon of Sichuan sauce.

물을 4컵 부은 후 쓰촨소스 1큰술을 넣어준다.

5 Add the mushrooms, tofu skin, fish balls, and Vienna sausages to the boiling broth and cook.

끓는 국물에 버섯, 푸주, 피시볼, 비엔나 소시지를 넣고 끓인다.

6 After it boils for a bit, add the bok choy, enoki mushrooms, and cilantro. Add udon noodles, then boil and serve in a bowl.

한소끔 끓고 나서 청경채, 팽이버섯, 고수를 넣고 우동면을 넣어서 끓인 후 그릇에 담는다.

Cook 02

Jisamsun

지삼선

Allergen Information	Spiciness Level	Way to Cook
 Bean	 Spicy	 Deep frying Pan frying
알러지 정보 콩	맵기 단계 신라면	조리 기법 튀김, 팬 프라잉

RECIPE

Ingredients(for 2 Servings)

Eggplant : 3
Sweet Potato : 2
Bell Pepper : 2
Cooking Oil : 800ml
Starch : 50g

재료(2인분)

가지 3개
고구마 2개
파프리카 2개
식용유 800ml
전분 50g

Broth

Soy Sauce : 3 tbsps
Oyster Sauce : 1 tbsp
Sugar : 1 tbsp
Vinegar : 1 tbsp
Doubanjiang : 0.5 tbsp
Minced Garlic : 1 tbsp
Minced Ginger : 1 tbsp
Green Onion : 20g
Starch Water(2 tsps starch) : 100ml

육수

간장 3큰술
굴소스 1큰술
설탕 1큰술
식초 1큰술
두반장 0.5큰술
다진 마늘 1큰술
다진 생강 1큰술
대파 20g
전분물(전분 2작은술) 100ml

Tip

- If the ingredient is wet, the starch may not stick well, so remove the moisture with a paper towel and apply the starch.
- When simmering the sauce, be careful with the heat, as it can burn if it's too high. Adjust the heat to medium-low.
- If the frying is not done crisply enough, the fried items may become soggy when mixed with the sauce, so make sure to fry them until crisp

- 물기가 묻으면 전분이 잘 안 묻을 수 있으므로 키친타월로 물기를 잘 제거하고 전분을 묻힌다.
- 소스를 끓일 때 불이 너무 세면 탈 수 있으므로 중약불을 잘 조절해야 한다.
- 튀김이 바삭하게 튀겨지지 않으면 소스를 버무릴 때 숨이 죽을 수가 있으니 바싹 튀기자.

PREPARATION

1 Cut the eggplant and the sweet potato into 3~4cm fan-shaped pieces.

가지와 고구마를 3~4cm 크기 부채꼴 모양으로 썬다.

2 Cut the paprika into 3cm cubes.

파프리카는 3cm 크기로 깍둑썬다.

③ Chop the green onions.

파를 썬다.

④ Mix the sauce.

소스를 섞는다.

COOKING STEPS

① Coat the eggplant, sweet potato, and paprika evenly with starch.

가지, 고구마, 파프리카에 전분을 골고루 입혀준다.

② Deep-fry the eggplant and vegetables in oil heated to 180°C.

180도 기름에서 가지와 야채를 튀겨준다.

③ In a preheated pan, add oil and saute the green onions first, then add the garlic and ginger, and cook until they turn brown. Pour in the sauce and simmer.

예열된 팬에 기름을 두르고 파를 먼저 볶다가 마늘, 생강을 갈색빛이 날 때까지 볶은 후 소스를 붓고 졸인다.

4 Add the starch water and adjust the thickness to your liking. Once the sauce thickens, add the pre-fried items and mix thoroughly to coat.

전분물을 넣고 농도를 걸쭉하게 맞춘 다음, 졸여진 소스에 미리 튀긴 튀김들을 넣고 골고루 버무리면 완성!

5 Place it nicely in a bowl.

그릇에 예쁘게 담아준다.

Episode 08

For SKT T1 Legends Bang and Wolf
안심 스테이크 & 라구 파스타 – 뱅과 울프 선수를 위하여

Tenderloin Steak & Ragu Pasta

Date Jan 10, 2022

Introduction Special meal provided to honor the retirement of SKT T1 legends Bang and Wolf

일자 2022. 1. 10
소개 SKT T1 레전드 뱅과 울프 선수의 은퇴식을 맞이하여 제공된 특별한 식사

STORY

Retirement Ceremony at the Headquarters!

Bang & Wolf are teammates and a legendary Bottom duo who, in 2015 and 2016, lifted the League of Legends World Championship trophies alongside Faker. When I heard that they would be holding their retirement ceremony at the T1 headquarters, I couldn't just stand by.

I asked if they would be eating out before the retirement ceremony, and luckily, I found out they'd be having the meal at the headquarters. I mentioned to the team preparing for the ceremony that I'd like to prepare the meal, and once I got the go-ahead, the cooking mode started in full gear.

Having filmed content with Wolf several times, I knew he was allergic to cucumbers, shrimp, and crab. Considering Bang's allergies as well, I excluded ingredients that could cause allergic reactions.

은퇴식을 사옥에서!

뱅 & 울프 선수는 2015년과 2016년에 페이커 선수와 롤드컵 우승컵을 2년 연속 들어올린 동료이자 레전드 바텀듀오다. 그들이 은퇴식을 T1 사옥에서 진행한다는 소식을 듣고 가만히 있을 수 없었다. 은퇴식 전에 혹시 외부에서 식사를 하는지 알아보았다. 다행히 사옥에서 식사를 한다는 얘기를 전달받았다. 은퇴식을 준비하는 부서에 특식을 대접하고 싶다는 의사를 타진했다. OK 화답을 받고 나자 본격적으로 쿠킹 회로가 돌아갔다.

울프 선수와는 몇 차례 콘텐츠도 찍은 터라 오이, 새우, 게 알레르기가 있다는 사실을 알고 있었다. 뱅 선수까지 고려해 알레르기를 유발하는 재료를 배제했다.

As a result, it was decided: meat! 'When it comes to meat, nothing beats a tender steak. And adding a rich ragu pasta with plenty of beef and pork will make the perfect dish to send off these two legends.'

I set up two seats in the restaurant area. I confirmed the visiting time, boiled the sauce, and prepared the noodles in advance. I grilled the meat 10 minutes before serving, allowed it to rest, and then prepared it to be served on a heated cast-iron pan. I was thankful that they enjoyed their meal, but instead, I was told, "Thank you, Chef." Thanks to the two players, I now have the honor of having such a memorable experience, preparing the final meal for legends.

그 결과 고기로 낙점! '고기 하면 안심 스테이크가 최고지. 소고기와 돼지고기가 듬뿍 들어간 라구 파스타까지 곁들이면 두 레전드를 환송하는 최고의 음식 조합이 되리라' 식당 온실 구역에 두 자리를 세팅했다. 방문 시간을 확인해 소스를 끓이고 면을 삶아 두었다. 고기는 10분 전에 구워서 레스팅까지 마친 후 달군 무쇠팬에 나갈 준비를 마쳤다. 맛있게 먹어주어 감사한데, 되려 "셰프님 감사합니다"라는 말을 들었다. 두 선수 덕분에 레전드의 마지막 식사를 챙길 수 있는 영광스러운 추억을 갖게 되었다.

Bae 'Bang' Jun-sik
'뱅' 배준식

Lee 'Wolf' Jae-wan
'울프' 이재완

When you watch football or baseball, don't they often have retirement ceremonies or farewell games? The retirement ceremonies of these two players have set a wonderful precedent in the esports industry, and as someone working in the field, I feel proud. I hope other players also have an honorable career and a memorable retirement ceremony… And every time, I will send them off with the best food.

축구나 야구를 보면 은퇴식이나 은퇴경기를 하지 않던가? 두 선수의 은퇴식은 e스포츠 업계에 멋진 선례를 만든 것 같아, 업계 종사자로서 뿌듯하다. 다른 선수들도 영광스러운 현역 시절을 보내고 기억에 남을 은퇴식을 갖기를… 그때마다 나는 최고의 음식으로 환송할 것이다.

About the Dish

Tenderloin steak is a steak made from the tenderloin (fillet), which is the inner part of the cow's waist. It has a soft texture and a mild taste due to its low fat content. It is considered a high-quality cut, and it is usually cooked to medium rare to preserve its soft texture.

Ragu pasta is a dish where a traditional Italian sauce, 'ragu,' made by simmering minced meat and vegetables in a rich tomato sauce, is served with pasta. It's also known as bolognese sauce, and its rich umami and deep flavors have made it a beloved dish over time.

음식 소개

안심 스테이크는 소의 허리 안쪽 부위인 안심(필레)을 사용한 스테이크로, 육질이 부드럽고 지방 함량이 적어 담백한 맛을 낸다. 고급 부위로 여겨지며, 미디엄 레어 정도로 조리해 부드러운 식감을 살리는 것이 일반적이다.

라구 파스타는 토마토 소스에 다진 고기와 채소를 오래 끓여 진한 풍미를 낸 이탈리아 전통 소스 '라구'를 파스타 면과 함께 즐기는 요리다. 볼로네제 소스라고도 불리며, 풍부한 감칠맛과 깊은 맛으로 꾸준한 사랑을 받고 있다.

Cook 01

Tenderloin Steak

안심 스테이크

Allergen Information   **Spiciness Level**   **Way to Cook**

Wheat Celery Pork   Mild   Pan frying

알러지 정보 밀, 셀러리, 돼지고기   맵기 단계 순한맛   조리 기법 팬 프라잉

RECIPE

 Ingredients (for 2 Servings)

Tenderloin : 200g
Salt : 1 tsp
Pepper : a little
Cooking Oil : 3 tbsps
Butter : 80g
Whole Garlic : 5
Rosemary : 1 sprig

재료 (2인분)

안심 200g
소금 1작은술
후추 약간
식용유 3큰술
버터 80g
통마늘 5개
로즈마리 1줄기

 Sauce

Grape Juice : 100ml
Onion : 80g
Sugar : 1 tbsp
Chicken Stock : 1 tbsp
Bay Leaves : 3
Rosemary : 1 sprig

소스

포도주스 100ml
양파 80g
설탕 1큰술
치킨스톡 1큰술
월계수잎 3장
로즈마리 1줄기

 **Tip**

- Since tenderloin has little fat, it becomes tough and dry if cooked for a long time. So it is recommended to cook it medium.
- For plating, you can use sauce, purée, and garnish to create a beautiful presentation.
- If the tenderloin is frozen, thaw it in the fridge for about 6 hours before using.
- Take the tenderloin out of the fridge 30 minutes before cooking to let it come to room temperature.

- 안심은 비계가 적어 오래 구우면 질겨지고 퍽퍽해지므로 미디엄으로 굽는 걸 추천한다.
- 플레이팅할 때 소스, 퓌레, 가니쉬를 활용해 이쁘게 꾸밀 수 있다.
- 안심이 냉동일 때는 냉장실에서 6시간 정도 해동 후 사용하면 된다.
- 안심은 굽기 30분 전에 실온에 꺼내두자.

PREPARATION

1 Season both sides of the meat with salt and pepper after removing any excess blood. Then tie the sides with string.

핏기를 제거한 고기 양면에 소금, 후추를 뿌려 밑간을 해준 후 실로 옆면을 묶어준다.

2 Cut the onion into 0.2cm pieces.

양파를 0.2cm 두께로 채썬다.

COOKING STEPS

1 Preheat a pan and add some cooking oil.

팬을 예열하고 식용유을 뿌린다.

2 Heat the pan until it's hot enough to make a sizzling sound when the meat is placed in it. Place the meat in the pan, then lower the heat and cook for another minute.

고기를 올렸을 때 '치익' 소리가 날 정도로 팬을 달궈준다. 고기를 올려두고 불을 낮춰 또 1분간 굽는다.

3 Flip the meat over, add butter, and cook again on high heat for about 30 seconds.

고기를 뒤집은 뒤 버터를 넣고 다시 강불에서 약 30초간 굽는다.

4 Reduce the heat to low and baste the meat with butter, cooking for about 1 minute 30 seconds to 2 minutes.

다시 약불로 낮춰 버터를 고기에 끼얹으며 약 1분 30초~2분간 구워준다.

5. Place it on the drain and rest for 5 to 6 minutes.

   드레인에 올려 5~6분 레스팅해준다.

6. Add butter to the pan you cooked the meat in, stir-fry the onion, add the mixed sauce, and simmer.

   고기를 구웠던 팬에 버터를 넣고 양파를 볶아준 후 섞은 소스를 넣고 졸인다.

7. Place the rested meat on a plate and plate the simmered sauce on top of the meat.

   레스팅된 고기를 접시에 담고 고기 위에 소스를 뿌려 플레이팅한다.

Cook 02

Ragu Pasta

라구 파스타

Allergen Information

 Wheat
 Celery
 Pork
 Beef

Spiciness Level

 Mild

Way to Cook

 Boiling
 Pan frying

알러지 정보 밀, 셀러리, 돼지고기, 소고기   맵기 단계 순한맛   조리 기법 끓이기, 팬 프라잉

RECIPE

Ingredients (for 2 Servings)
Fettuccine Pasta : 180g
Grana Padano Cheese : a little
Cooking Oil : a little

재료(2인분)
페투치네면 180g
그라나파다노치즈 약간
식용유 약간

Sauce
Ground Pork : 100g
Ground Beef : 150g
Tomato : 250g
Tomato Paste : 100g
Chicken Stock : 50g
Onion : 150g
Carrot : 0.5
Celery : 1 stalk
Bay Leaves : 3
Pepper : a little
Salt : a little
Minced Garlic : 1 tsp
Butter : 30g
Fresh Basil : 1g

소스
돼지다짐육 100g
소고기다짐육 150g
토마토 250g
토마토페이스트 100g
치킨스톡 50g
양파 150g
당근 0.5개
샐러리 1줄기
월계수잎 3장
후추 약간
소금 약간
다진 마늘 1작은술
버터 30g
생바질 1g

Tip
- Stir well to prevent the tomato sauce from burning.
- If you want to lessen the sourness, add a small amount of sugar.
- Be sure to add salt to the water when cooking the pasta so the pasta absorbs the flavor well.
- After finishing the sauce, adding a piece of butter will enhance the flavor.
- When adding pasta water, do it gradually, little by little, while checking the consistency.

- 잘 저어줘야 토마토소스가 타지 않는다.
- 신맛을 줄이고 싶다면 설탕을 소량 넣자.
- 파스타면을 삶을 때 물에 소금을 넣어야 파스타면에 간이 잘 밴다.
- 소스를 완성시킨 후 버터 한 조각을 넣어주면 풍미가 더 좋아진다.
- 면수 넣을 때는 조금씩 농도를 봐가며 넣어준다.

PREPARATION

① Chop the onion and carrot into 0.2cm pieces.

양파와 당근을 0.2cm 크기로 잘게 다진다.

② Chop the celery into 0.2cm pieces after removing the fiber.

샐러리는 섬유질을 제거 후 0.2cm 크기로 다진다.

3. Make an x-shaped silt on the tomato with a knife, then blanch them in boiling water and then soak them in cold water.

   십자 모양으로 칼집을 내서 토마토를 끓는 물에 데쳤다가 찬 물에 담가둔다.

4. Peel and chop them.

   껍질을 벗긴 후 다진다.

5. Add bay leaves, pepper, salt, and chicken stock to the sauce and bring to a simmer.

   소스에 월계수잎, 후추, 소금, 치킨스톡을 넣고 끓인다.

6. In a preheated pan, add the pasta and saute, coating it evenly. Add the pre-made sauce to the pan and stir, gradually adding the reserved pasta water to adjust the consistency, then season with salt.

   예열된 팬에 파스타면을 넣고 코팅하듯이 볶는다. 미리 만들어둔 소스를 팬에 적당량 넣고 볶다가 면수를 넣어가며 농도를 맞추고 소금으로 간을 맞춘다.

7 Serve on a plate.

접시에 플레이팅한다.

Episode 09

Jangeodeopbap
—Grilled Eel with Rice

Ahead of the LCK Spring Finals

장어덮밥 – LCK 스프링 결승전을 앞두고

Date	Apr 1, 2022
Introduction	Our players have worked hard during the spring season! We have prepared a special meal to help them recover their energy before the finals.
Allergen Information	Fish, Egg
Spiciness Level	Mild
Way to Cook	Steaming, Braising, Pan-frying

일자	2022. 4. 1
소개	스프링 시즌 고생한 우리 선수들! 결승전을 앞두고 원기 회복하라고 특식을 마련했다.
알러지 정보	생선, 계란
맵기 단계	순한맛
조리 기법	찌기, 볶음찜, 팬 프라잉

RECIPE

 Ingredients(for 2 Servings)

Freshwater Eel : 500g
Eggs : 3
Salt : a little
Perilla Leaves : 5g
Rice : 200g

재료(2인분)

민물장어 500g
계란 3개
소금 약간
깻잎 5g
밥 200g

 Sauce

Soy Sauce : 90ml
Cheongju(Korean Rice Wine) : 90ml
Mirin : 90ml
Sugar : 70ml
Water(Dashi Stock) : 90ml
Green Onion : 100g
Onion : 150g
Garlic : 40g
Ginger : 10g
Red Chili Pepper : 1

소스

간장 90ml
청주 90ml
맛술 90ml
설탕 70ml
물(다시물) 90ml
대파 100g
양파 150g
마늘 40g
생강 10g
홍고추 1개

 Tip

- Boil the kombu and bonito flakes in boiling water for about 5 minutes, then strain it to make dashi stock.
- If you prefer a softer texture, mix the teriyaki sauce with water in a 1:1 ratio, then simmer the steamed eel gently before placing it on top of the rice.
- Teriyaki sauce pairs well with chicken, pork, and beef. Make a batch and enjoy with various Japanese rice bowls. It can be stored in the fridge for up to 5 days.

- 끓는 물에 다시마와 가다랑어포를 5분간 끓이다가 건져주면 다시물이 된다.
- 부드러운 식감을 선호한다면 데리야끼 소스와 물을 1:1 비율로 맞춘 다음 찐 장어를 은근히 졸인 후에 밥 위에 얹어 먹자.
- 데리야끼 소스는 닭, 돼지, 소고기에 다 어울린다. 만들어두었다가 다양한 일식 덮밥을 즐겨보자. 냉장보관을 하면 5일 정도는 먹을 수 있다.

PREPARATION

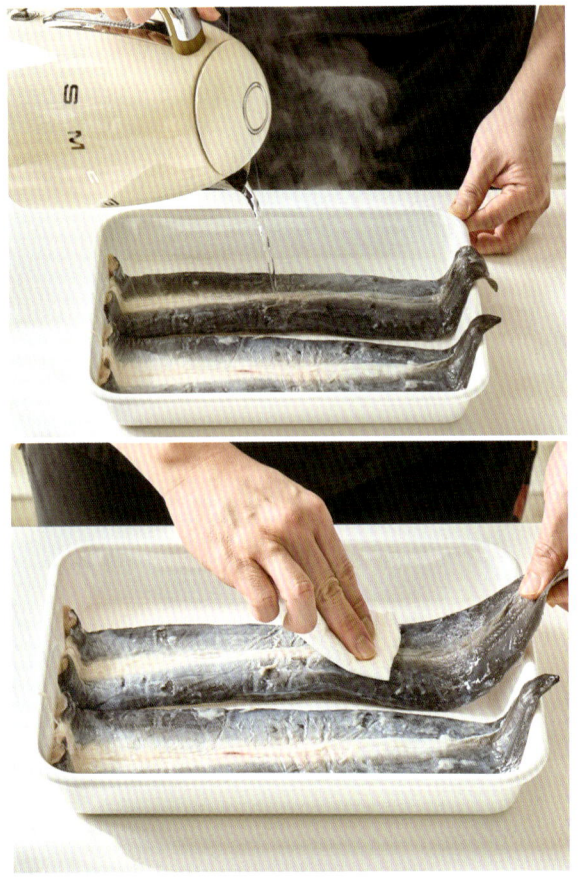

1 Pour hot water on the eel skin and wipe it with a paper towel.

뜨거운 물을 장어 껍질 쪽에 부어준 후 키친타월로 닦아낸다.

2 Cut the onion and green onion into 6 pieces.

양파, 대파를 6등분으로 썬다.

3 Slice the garlic and ginger.

마늘과 생강을 편으로 썬다.

4 Cut the perilla leaves into strips.

깻잎을 채썰어둔다.

COOKING STEPS

1 Cut the eel in half pieces and season with salt.

장어를 절반 크기로 썬 후 소금으로 밑간을 한다.

2 Line a steamer with a cloth, and once the water begins to boil, place the seasoned eel on top and steam for 20 minutes.

찜기에 면포를 깔고 물이 끓을 때 쯤 밑간한 장어를 올려 20분간 쪄낸다.

③ In an ungreased pan, slowly stir-fry the onion, green onion, garlic, ginger, and chili pepper over low heat with a spatula. When the aroma begins to rise, add the sauce ingredients and simmer for 5 minutes.

기름칠 안 한 팬에 양파, 대파, 마늘, 생강, 고추를 약불에서 천천히 주걱으로 볶은 다음 어느 정도 향이 올라오면 소스를 같이 넣고 5분간 끓인다.

④ Make an egg sheet using only the egg yolks, then let it cool and slice it thinly.

계란에 노른자만을 이용해 지단을 만든 후, 식힌 다음 채썰어 놓는다.

COOKING STEPS

5 In a pan, add oil and cook the steamed eel, starting with the skin side down over medium-low heat. Once it's somewhat cooked, flip it over.

팬에 기름을 두르고 찐 장어를 중약불에서 껍질 쪽부터 굽고, 어느 정도 익으면 뒤집는다.

6 Once the eel is golden brown, reduce the heat to low and evenly drizzle about 4 tablespoons of the pre-made teriyaki sauce over it. When the sauce thickens, brush it onto both sides of the eel with a brush.

장어가 노릇하게 구워졌으면 약불로 줄이고 미리 만들어둔 데리야끼 소스를 4큰술 정도 장어 위에 골고루 뿌려준다. 소스가 걸쭉해지면 솔을 이용해 장어 앞뒤로 발라준다.

7 Place the grilled eel on a strainer and heat it again with a torch to create a caramelizing effect. This process will give it a smoky flavor and aroma.

구운 장어를 거름망에 올리고 토치로 한 번 더 가열해가면서 캐러멜라이징 효과를 낸다. 이 작업으로 불맛과 향을 얻을 수 있다.

8 Drizzle 1–2 tablespoons of teriyaki sauce over the rice, place the egg sheet on top, followed by the grilled eel cut into thirds, and finish with perilla leaves.

밥 위에 데리야끼 소스 1~2큰술을 먼저 뿌려주고, 지단을 올리고, 그위에 3등분한 구운장어, 깻잎 순으로 올려 마무리한다.

Episode 10

Feijoada & Moqueca

Date	May 19, 2023
Introduction	A taste of home for the players from Brazil, and a new culinary experience for us!

일자	2023. 5. 19
소개	브라질에서 온 선수들에게 고향의 맛을, 우리에게 새로운 음식 체험을!

Taste Brazil's Hometown Food

페이조아다 & 모케카
– 브라질 고향 음식을 맛보세요

STORY

Is there such a thing as a training camp in eSports? T1A(T1 Esports Academy) runs a bootcamp that closely resembles what you'd find in traditional sports. Professional teams from North America, Europe, South America, and various Asian countries participate, staying for as short as a week or as long as a month. During this time, they train in the very same practice rooms and accommodations that T1 players use. They also experience every aspect of T1's environment, including rest areas, and even have the chance to scrim against the T1 squad. Thanks to its popularity, numerous teams apply and are eager to attend.

This bootcamp is an important event for me as well. Naturally, players from all over the world have distinct tastes, dietary restrictions, allergies, and religious considerations. For some, I've even arranged halal-certified ingredient suppliers to meet their specific needs.

While most of the meals served are Korean, I can't just offer only Korean cuisine to guests who have traveled so far. That's why I always include dishes like Korean BBQ, samgyeopsal, and galbi—items that foreigners tend to enjoy without much hesitation.

e스포츠에도 전지훈련이 있을까? T1 e스포츠 아카데미(T1A)는 부트캠프를 진행하는데, 타 스포츠에서 말하는 전지훈련과 비슷하다. 북미, 유럽, 남미, 아시아 여러 나라에서 프로팀이 짧게는 일주일, 길게는 한 달 동안 프로그램에 동참한다. 그 기간 T1 선수들이 실제로 사용하는 연습실이나 숙소에서 훈련한다. 또한 휴식공간 같은 T1의 모든 환경을 경험하고 T1 선수들과 스크림을 진행하기도 한다. 인기가 많아 많은 팀이 지원한다. 부트캠프는 나에게도 중요한 이벤트다. 전 세계에서 몰려든 선수 개개인의 입맛뿐 아니라 알레르기나 종교도 고려해야 한다. 한번은 할랄 식재료 납품 업체를 미리 선별해 제공하기도 했다.

대부분 식사 메뉴는 한식이지만, 멀리서 온 손님에게 한식만 대접할 수는 없는 노릇이다. 그래서 한식 중에서도 외국인도 무난하게 먹을 수 있는 코리안 BBQ, 삼겹살, 갈비를 빠지지 않고 내놓고 있다.

Once, a League of Legends team from Brazil, a country literally on the opposite side of the globe, joined our bootcamp for a fairly long stint. Since Brazil's official language is Portuguese, I tried learning a few simple greetings and phrases to check on their comfort at mealtimes. Fortunately, their manager spoke English, so we managed communication without resorting to Portuguese. (Phew, what a relief!)

When I think of Brazil, I think of samba, soccer, and passion—and my encounters didn't contradict those images. I still recall how warmly they greeted us with bright smiles. The first Korean dish they tried was jeyuk-bokkeum (spicy stir-fried pork). To accommodate their tastes, I toned down the heat, using just enough chili powder for a hint of color rather than full-fledged spiciness. Did it work? They joyfully exclaimed "Tá bom!" mixing the pork with rice and savoring it enthusiastically. Just to be safe, I asked their manager if it was too spicy or if there were any issues, but he simply said, "No problem! So good!"

Time flew by, and before I knew it, a month had passed since our first meeting. Over that time, I grew fond of a few players. We exchanged Instagram handles and followed each other. Then, I decided to bring out my secret weapon: feijoada & moqueca!

한 번은 지구 반대편 나라 브라질의 LoL팀이 꽤 오랜 기간 부트캠프에 참여했다. 찾아보니 브라질은 포르투갈어를 썼다. 포르투갈어로 간단한 인사와 식사에 불편함이 없는지 물어보는 공부를 해뒀다. 다행히 담당 매니저가 영어를 사용해 포르투갈어를 사용하지 않고도 소통을 할 수 있었다. (휴~ 다행이다!) 브라질 하면 삼바 댄스와 축구, 그리고 열정이 떠오른다. 만나보니 내 선입견이 틀리지 않았다. 환하게 웃으며 인사를 건네준 브라질팀의 모습은 지금 생각해도 정겹다. 그들에게 처음 선보인 음식은 제육볶음이었다. 브라질 선수단을 고려해 맵기를 조절해서 색깔만 낼 정도로 고춧가루를 사용했다. 맵기 조절이 통한 건가! "따봉"을 외치며 밥을 비벼서 너무 맛있게 먹는 것이다.

그래도 노파심에 매니저에게 맵거나 불편한 사항이 없는지 체크했지만 "No problem! So good!" 이렇게 첫 만남 후 한 달이 후딱 지났다. 알게 모르게 정이 쌓인 선수도 있었다. 인스타를 물어보고 서로 맞팔을 했다. 그리고 비장의 무기를 꺼내들었다. 바로 페이조아다 & 모케카!

STORY

I first tasted these dishes five years ago at a world food culture festival in Seoul. I had kept the recipes ever since, and now I finally had the chance to serve them to actual Brazilians. When I told them, "We'll be serving feijoada for your farewell meal," they responded once again with "Tá bom!" Although the appearance of feijoada might look unfamiliar, it's somewhat reminiscent of Korea's budae-jjigae (army stew). If you ever have the chance, I highly recommend giving it a try.

이 음식은 5년 전에, 서울시에서 개최한 세계 음식 문화 축제에서 처음 맛봤다. 그당시 레시피를 만들어놓았는데 이렇게 현지인에게 선보일 날이 오다니... 브라질 선수들에게 "페이조아다를 마지막 식사로 준비할 거예요!"라고 말하자 역시 "따봉"으로 화답한다. 페이조아다의 비주얼은 낯설지만, 우리나라 부대찌개와 닮았다. 기회가 되면 한번 도전해보기 바란다.

About the Dish

Feijoada is a traditional Brazilian stew made by slowly simmering black beans with pork and sausages. It has a rich, savory flavor and is commonly enjoyed with rice and farofa (toasted manioc flour). Beloved for weekend family gatherings and national holidays, it's truly a signature Brazilian dish.

Moqueca is a Brazilian seafood stew cooked with fresh seafood, coconut milk, tomatoes, onions, and bell peppers. Its smooth texture and the harmonious blend of tropical flavors and spices give it an exotic character. Celebrated in coastal regions, it's a widely loved staple of Brazil's culinary heritage.

음식 소개

페이조아다는 검은콩과 돼지고기, 소시지 등을 푹 끓여낸 브라질 전통 스튜로, 고소하고 진한 풍미를 자랑한다. 쌀밥, 파우파르파(마니옥 가루)와 함께 즐기며, 국경일이나 주말가족식사로 사랑받는 대표 음식이다.

모케카는 신선한 해산물을 코코넛 밀크, 토마토, 양파, 피망 등과 함께 조린 브라질식 해산물 스튜다. 부드러운 식감과 열대 과일, 향신료의 조화가 이국적이다. 해안 지방 전통 음식으로 널리 알려져 있다.

Cook 01

Feijoada

페이조아다

Allergen Information

Peanuts

Soy

Wheat

Pork

알러지 정보 땅콩, 대두, 밀, 돼지고기

Spiciness Level

Mild

맵기 단계 순한맛

Way to Cook

Pan frying

조리 기법 팬 프라잉

RECIPE

Ingredients(for 2 Servings)

Pork Shoulder : 300g
Thick Bacon : 100g
Sausage : 120g
Onion : 400g
Garlic : 15g
Bay Leaves : 3
Salt : a little
Water : 600ml
Green Beans : 200g
Butter Beans : 200g
Cooking Oil : 50ml

재료(2인분)

돼지 앞다리살 300g
두꺼운 베이컨 100g
소시지 120g
양파 400g
마늘 15g
월계수잎 3장
소금 약간
물 600ml
강낭콩 200g
버터빈스 200g
식용유 50ml

Tip

- Normally, ribs or thick stewing cuts of meat are used, but I used shoulder meat to save on cooking time.
- It also goes well with pasta when you add tomatoes.

- 원래는 갈비나 두꺼운 찜용 고기를 쓰지만 조리 시간 절약을 위하여 앞다리살을 활용했다.
- 토마토를 같이 넣고 파스타를 활용해도 잘 어울린다.

PREPARATION

1 Cut the bacon into 2cm thick pieces and the sausage into 2cm thick pieces.

베이컨을 2cm, 소시지를 2cm 두께로 어슷썬다.

2 Slice the onion into 1cm thick slices.

양파를 1cm 두께로 슬라이스한다.

3 Slice the garlic into slices.

마늘을 편으로 썰어준다.

COOKING STEPS

1 Add cooking oil to a preheated pan and fry the bacon first, then fry the sausage and set aside.

예열한 팬에 식용유를 두르고 베이컨을 먼저 볶고, 소시지를 볶은 후 건져놓는다.

2 In the same pan, add a little oil and fry the garlic and onion until they become translucent, then add the pork and fry until they turn brown.

같은 팬에 기름을 약간만 넣고 마늘, 양파를 볶다가 투명해지면 돼지고기를 넣고 갈색빛이 날 때까지 볶는다.

3 Add the beans that have been drained in advance, and add the bay leaves and water.

미리 물기를 제거한 콩을 같이 넣어주고 월계수잎과 물을 넣어준다.

4 When it starts to boil, add the fried sausage and bacon together and simmer over low heat.

끓기 시작하면 볶아놓은 소시지와 베이컨을 같이 넣고 약불로 졸여준다.

5 When the broth is almost done, turn off the heat and pour into a bowl.

국물이 자작해지면 불을 끄고 그릇에 담는다.

Cook 02

Moqueca

모케카

Allergen Information

Shrimp

알러지 정보 새우

Spiciness Level

Mild

맵기 단계 순한맛

Way to Cook

Boiling

조리 기법 끓이기

RECIPE

Ingredients(for 4 Servings)

Shrimp : 600g
Onion : 400g
Tomato : 450g
Bell Pepper : 200g
Lime : 1
Red Chili Pepper : 1
Minced Garlic : 4 tbsps
Coconut Milk : 500ml
Tomato Paste : 2 tbsps
Salt : a little
Pepper : a little
Parsley : a little
Green Onion : 100g
Cooking Oil : 80ml

재료(4인분)

새우 600g
양파 400g
토마토 450g
파프리카 200g
라임 1개
홍고추 1개
다진 마늘 4큰술
코코넛밀크 500ml
토마토페이스트 2큰술
소금 약간
후추 약간
파슬리 약간
쪽파 100g
식용유 80ml

Tip

- Add mussel broth to make it more like a stew.
- Adding more lime will give it a tom yum flavor.
- It pairs well with fried rice or fatty meats.

- 홍합 육수를 넣어 스튜처럼 만들 수도 있다.
- 라임을 많이 넣으면 똠얌꿍 맛이 난다.
- 볶음밥이나 기름진 고기와 곁들여 먹으면 조합이 좋다.

PREPARATION

1 Cut the onion and paprika into 1cm cubes.

양파, 파프리카를 1cm 크기로 깍둑 썬다.

2 Cut the tomato into 2cm cubes.

토마토를 2cm 크기로 깍둑 썬다.

3 Cut the red pepper into 0.2cm thick slices.

홍고추를 0.2cm 두께로 썰어준다.

4 Finely chop the green onion.

쪽파를 잘게 썬다.

COOKING STEPS

1 Put shrimp in a bowl, season with lime, garlic, and salt, and marinate for 20 minutes.

볼에 새우를 넣고 라임, 마늘, 소금으로 양념한 후 20분간 숙성시킨다.

2 Put oil in a pot, fry garlic first, fry onion and paprika, then fry tomato.

냄비에 오일을 두른 후 마늘을 먼저 볶고, 양파와 파프리카를 볶은 다음 토마토를 볶아준다.

③ Put marinated shrimp in the frying pot and lightly season with salt.

볶은 냄비 안에 숙성해둔 새우를 넣어주고 소금간을 살짝해준다.

④ Add tomato paste and stir-fry.

토마토페이스트를 넣고 볶아준다.

5 Add coconut milk to the pot.

냄비 안에 코코넛 밀크를 넣는다.

6 Add red chili and green onions, then cover and simmer on low heat for about 20 minutes until the shrimp is cooked. Stir well and season with salt to taste, and it's done!

홍고추, 쪽파를 넣고 새우가 익을 때까지 약불로 20분간 뚜껑을 닫고 끓인다. 그후 잘 저어준 후 소금으로 간을 맞추면 끝!

7 Serve on a plate

플레이팅한다.

Episode 11

Wanggalbitang

Nourishment for the Winter

왕갈비탕 – 겨울에는 음식이 보약

Date   Jan 15, 2022
Introduction   Making wanggalbitang straight out of a comic book!
Allergen Information   Beef
Spiciness Level   Mild
Way to Cook   Boiling

일자   2022. 1. 15
소개   만화에서 갑툭튀한 왕갈비탕 만들기!
알러지 정보   소고기
맵기 단계   순한맛
조리 기법   끓이기

I wasn't about to give up. Instead, I thought, why not tackle the problem at its root? "What if I do the butchering myself?" With that, I headed to a butcher shop, where I was recommended whole ribs that I could trim myself. It had been a while since I'd done such work, and it wasn't easy. Beef ribs are thick and hefty, making them tricky to shape. But the thought of serving this magnificent dish kept me motivated, and I completed the trimming process successfully.

The trimmed ribs were transformed into galbitang, with tender, sizable cuts of meat nestled in a clear, rich broth. The meat clinging to the bones would fall apart with the gentlest touch.

나는 포기하지 않았다. 오히려 더 근본적인 해결책을 찾기로 했다. '직접 정육을 하면 어떨까?' 나는 그 길로 정육점을 찾아갔다. 원물 그대로 갈비를 추천받고 정형하는 과정을 선택한 것이다. 오랜만에 하는 작업이라 쉽지는 않았다. 소갈비가 워낙 뼈도 크고 두꺼워서 모양 잡기가 쉽진 않았지만, 왕갈비를 대접할 즐거운 상상 덕분에 무사히 정육을 마칠 수 있었다.

정육을 마친 갈비는 갈비탕으로 재탄생했다. 고운 국물 속에 풍덩 담긴 큼직한 갈비, 그 뼈에 가득 붙은 고기는 입에 넣는 순간 부드럽게 풀어질 것이다.

Finally, the moment of truth arrived. As the employees entered the dining area, they were blown away by the impressive size and appearance of the galbitang. Like characters from a comic, they each took a sip of the broth, savoring the flavor, before grabbing the massive ribs and tearing into them. Bite after bite, they couldn't get enough. Watching them enjoy the meal so wholeheartedly, I felt an overwhelming sense of satisfaction—as though I had checked off a major item on my life bucket list.

드디어 개봉박두. 식당에 들어서는 직원들은 압도적인 갈비 사이즈와 비주얼에 다들 감탄사를 내뱉었다. 그리고 약속이나 한 듯이 만화 주인공처럼 국물 한 모금 음미하고 나서 커다란 갈비를 들고 뜯었다. 그리고 또 뜯고, 또 뜯었다. 그런 장면을 보고 있자니 인생 버킷 리스트 하나를 클리어한 뿌듯함이 밀려왔다.

About the Dish

Wanggalbitang is a traditional Korean soup made by simmering large beef short ribs until the broth is both clear and richly flavored. The combination of tender, slow-cooked rib meat and the clean, invigorating broth is exceptional. Mild and highly nutritious, it's often enjoyed as a restorative meal. Commonly, ingredients like green onion are added to enhance the flavor, and it is served with salt or pepper on the side to season to your taste.

음식 소개

왕갈비탕은 큼직한 소갈비를 푹 고아 맑고 진한 국물을 낸 한국 전통 탕요리다. 부드럽게 익은 갈비살과 시원한 육수의 조화가 일품이며, 담백하고 영양가가 풍부해 보양식으로 즐겨 먹는다. 대개 대파 등으로 맛을 더하며 소금이나 후추를 곁들여 개인 취향에 맞춰 먹는다.

PREPARATION

1. Soak the ribs in cold water for about an hour to remove the blood.

   찬물에 갈비를 담가 1시간 정도 핏물을 빼준다.

2. Slice the green onion and red chili into 0.2cm rounds.

   대파와 홍고추를 0.2cm 두께로 썬다.

3. Remove the seeds from the jujubes and cut them into 0.1cm thick slices.

   대추는 씨를 뺀 다음, 0.1cm 두께로 썬다.

4. Cut the egg yolk garnish into 0.3cm thick slices.

   지단을 0.3cm 두께로 채썬다.

COOKING STEPS

1 Soak the glass noodles in water.

당면을 불려놓는다.

2 Place the soaked ribs in a pot, fill with water until the ribs are submerged, and sprinkle coffee grounds. Boil for about 10 minutes.

냄비에 갈비를 넣고 고기가 잠길 정도로 물을 채우고 커피 가루를 뿌린 후 10분간 끓여준다.

③ Drain the boiled ribs and rinse thoroughly under cold water.

끓인 갈비를 채에 받쳐서 찬 물로 깨끗이 씻는다.

④ In a stockpot, add jujubes, radish, green onion, garlic, and whole peppercorns. Fill with water until the ribs are submerged and boil on high heat to make the broth.

냄비에 대추, 무, 대파, 마늘, 통후추를 넣고 갈비가 잠길 정도 물을 채워 강불에 끓여 육수를 낸다.

5 Skim off the fat floating on the surface. Once boiling, reduce to medium-low heat, cover, and simmer for 1 hour and 30 minutes.

물 위에 뜨는 기름을 잘 걷어낸다. 물이 끓기 시작하면 중약불로 1시간 30분간 뚜껑을 덮고 끓여준다.

6 Add 3 tablespoons of soy sauce, 1 tablespoon of salt, and a splash of cheongju, then simmer for another 30 minutes.

국간장 3큰술, 소금 1큰술, 청주를 넣고 30분 더 끓인다.

7 Remove the ribs and trim off any excess fat.

갈비를 덜어내고 지방을 제거한다.

8 Strain the broth through a strainer.

육수를 채로 거른다.

⑨ Adjust the seasoning of the broth with salt, pepper, and a pinch of sugar.

육수 간을 보고 소금, 후추를 적당량 넣고 설탕을 약간 넣어준다.

⑩ Place the ribs, green onion, sesame seeds, and jujube in a ttukbaegi, pour in the broth, and boil until done.

뚝배기에 갈비, 대파, 지단, 대추를 올려주고 자작하게 국물을 담고 끓이면 완성이다.

Episode 12

Hamburg Steak

A Special Dish for the Good Young Man on the Subway

함박 스테이크 – 지하철 착한 청년을 위한 특식

Date	Jul 25, 2023
Introduction	I invited a young man who was cleaning dirty seats in the subway.
Allergen Information	🥚 Eggs, 🐖 Pork, 🐄 Beef
Spiciness Level	🌶 Mild
Way to Cook	🍲 Stewing, 🍳 Pan-frying

일자	2023. 7. 25
소개	지하철에서 더럽혀진 좌석을 청소하던 바른 청년을 초대했다.
알러지 정보	계란, 돼지고기, 소고기
맵기 단계	순한맛
조리 기법	조림, 팬 프라잉

RECIPE

Ingredients (for 4 Servings)

Ground Beef : 250g
Ground Pork : 150g
Eggs : 6 / Onion : 150g
Celery : 100g
Breadcrumbs(fine) : 100g
Worcestershire Sauce : 30ml
A1 Steak Sauce : 30ml
Hot Sauce : 15ml
Minced Garlic : 1 tbsp
Salt : 1 tsp
Chicken Powder : 12g
Beef Powder : 12g
Cooking Oil : 3 tbsps
Glutinous Rice Flour : 20g
Sesame Oil : 50ml
Eggs : 4 / Parsley : a little

재료(4인분)

소고기다짐육 250g
돼지고기다짐육 150g
달걀 6개 / 양파 150g
샐러리 100g
빵가루(고운) 100g
우스터소스 30ml
A1스테이크소스 30ml
핫소스 15ml
다진 마늘 1큰술
소금 1작은술
치킨파우더 12g
비프파우더 12g
식용유 3큰술
찹쌀가루 20g
참기름 50ml
계란 4개 / 파슬리 약간

Sauce

Onion : 100g
Light Soy Sauce : 0.5 tbsp
Worcestershire Sauce : 0.5 tbsp
Ketchup : 3 tbsps
Butter : 50g / Pepper : a little
Water : 50ml / Sugar : 2 tbsps

소스

양파 100g
진간장 0.5큰술
우스터소스 0.5큰술
케첩 3큰술
버터 50g / 후추 약간
물 50ml / 설탕 2큰술

Tip

- The taste and texture of a hamburg steak vary greatly depending on the meat ratio. A lower ratio gives a softer texture, while a higher ratio results in a firmer bite.
- You can substitute the sauce with demi-glace sauce for a smooth and rich hamburg steak.
- It also pairs wonderfully with tomato pasta.
- Add cheese, pickles, onion, and tomato on bread to make a homemade hamburg steak burger.
- When kneading, be sure to do it thoroughly to remove the air trapped in the meat. Skipping this step can cause the meat to crack or fall apart while grilling.

- 함박 스테이크는 고기 비율에 따라 맛과 식감이 천차 만별이다. 비율이 낮으면 부드러운 식감이고, 비율이 높으면 상대적으로 단단한 식감이 된다.
- 데미글라스소스로 대체해도 부드럽고 고소한 함박 스테이크를 먹을 수 있다.
- 토마토 파스타와 곁들여 먹어도 맛이 어울린다.
- 빵에 치즈와 피클, 양파, 토마토를 곁들여 먹으면 수제 함박 스테이크 버거가 된다.
- 반죽을 할 때 제대로 치대야 고기 사이 공기가 빠진다. 이 작업을 소홀히 하면 구울 때 고기가 갈라지거나 부서진다.

PREPARATION

1 Chop the onion and celery into 0.2cm thick pieces.

양파, 샐러리를 0.2cm 두께로 다져준다.

2 Mix the onion, soy sauce, Worcestershire sauce, ketchup, butter, pepper, water, and sugar to make the sauce.

양파, 진간장, 우스터소스, 케첩, 버터, 후추, 물, 설탕을 섞어 소스를 만든다.

COOKING STEPS

1 Without adding oil, saute the onion and celery in a pan with salt and pepper, then let them cool.

양파, 샐러리를 기름 없이 팬에 소금, 후추를 뿌려 볶고 나서 식혀둔다.

2 Mix the sauce with the cooked onion and celery.

소스를 고기랑 미리 볶은 양파, 샐러리랑 혼합하여 준다.

3 Shape the mixture into 130g portions and form them into baseball-sized patties.

무게 130g짜리 야구공 모양으로 만든다.

4 To prevent breaking, repeatedly knead the patties to remove air, then shape them into flat rounds and place them on a plate.

만들어진 함박은 공기를 빼야 안 깨지므로 여러 번 치댄 다음 넙적한 모양으로 만들어 접시에 올려놓는다.

5 Preheat a pan over high heat, add oil, and carefully place the patties in the pan.

강불로 예열한 팬에 기름을 두르고 함박을 천천히 올려놓는다.

6 Once browned, gently flip the patties, add a small amount of water, reduce the heat to low, cover the pan, and cook for about 8 minutes.

노릇하게 구워지면 천천히 뒤집은 뒤 소량의 물을 넣고 약불로 불을 줄이고 뚜껑을 닫고 8분간 익혀준다.

7 In a preheated pan, stir-fry the onion with butter, salt, and pepper.

예열된 팬에 버터와 양파와 소금, 후추를 넣고 볶는다.

8 Once the onion turns brown, add the remaining sauce ingredients and simmer over low heat, stirring well. When the sauce thickens, turn off the heat.

양파가 갈색빛이 돌면 나머지 소스 재료들을 넣고 잘 저으며 약불로 끓인다. 진득하게 되면 불을 끈다.

9 Fry an egg to a soft-boiled consistency to top the patty.

함박 위에 올라갈 계란 후라이를 반숙으로 익혀준다.

10 Place the cooked patty on a plate, pour the sauce over it, top with the fried egg, and sprinkle with parsley to finish.

완성된 함박을 접시 위에 올려놓고 소스를 얹고 마지막에 계란 후라이를 얹고 파슬리를 뿌려 마무리한다.

Episode 13

Date	Jun 29, 2024
Introduction	On T1's first home ground event day, the TBap chefs headed out with hot dogs! The hot dogs were prepared to cook on-site.
Allergen Information	🥚 Egg, 🌾 Wheat, 🐖 Pork
Spiciness Level	🌶 Mild
Way to Cook	🍲 Boiling

일자	2024. 6. 29
소개	T1의 첫 홈그라운 행사날 티밥 셰프들이 핫도그를 들고 출격하다! 현장에서 조리 가능하게 준비해갔다.
알러지 정보	계란, 밀, 돼지고기
맵기 단계	순한맛
조리 기법	끓이기

STORY

Will the TChefs travel with the team for away games?
The TChef is not only the chef for the players, but also for the entire T1 family. While the players are the main focus, there are also T1 staff members working in the office who need meals. Therefore, the chefs don't travel to the stadium to provide meals during every game.
But in late June 2024, on the cusp of summer, T1 held its very first official LCK home-ground match. For this historic moment, the TChefs made an exception and decided to join the team. Briefly, I was excited at the thought of potentially watching the match in person. However, it was short-lived—first, we needed to check if we could actually cook on-site.
The on-site inspection revealed that cooking wasn't possible there. Determined not to give up, I searched for a menu perfectly suited to the environment.

티셰프는 선수단과 함께 원정 경기에 참여할까?
티셰프는 선수단뿐 아니라, T1 가족 모두의 셰프다. 선수단 말고도 늘 사무실에서 일하는 T1 직원들이 있기 때문에 경기가 있다고 해서 경기장까지 따라가서 식사를 제공하지는 않는다.
2024년 6월 말, 여름의 문턱에 서 있을 때였다. T1이 LCK 공식 경기로는 처음으로 홈그라운드 경기를 치르게 되었다. 예외로, 그 역사적인 순간에 티셰프들도 함께 하기로 했다. 현장에서 경기를 볼 수 있겠다는 설렘도 잠시! 우선 조리가 가능한 상황인지 현장 답사가 필요했다.
답사 결과 조리가 불가능한 상황임을 알게 되었다.
포기할 수 없었기에 현장 상황에 최적화된 메뉴를 찾던 끝에 미국식 핫도그로 정했다.

The solution? American-style hot dogs. After preparing all the ingredients in advance, we decided to run two booths offering five different flavors of hot dogs.

Despite the early, humid morning, fans crowded the venue, and their enthusiasm fueled my energy. The turnout was so immense that after just five hours, everything we had prepared sold out.

On that day, it wasn't just the chefs who contributed to the success of the event. T1 colleagues helped with the payment process, while others were running around, sweating, without even having time for a proper meal. One colleague's promise before the hot dog operation started — "Even if my face gets sunburned, I'll smile and finish the event safely" — still sticks in my mind. Without these precious colleagues, this mission would have been impossible. I am incredibly thankful.

As we look ahead to the next home ground event in 2025, I will cherish today's experience and continue to prepare even more thoroughly in the future.

재료를 사전에 모두 손질해 가서 두 개의 부스에서 5가지 맛 핫도그를 선보이기로 했다.

이른 아침부터 습한 날씨에도 불구하고 팬들이 몰려들었다. 그 수만큼 나도 힘이 났다. 너무나 많은 인파에 운영 5시간 만에 준비한 식재료가 모두 소진되고 말았다.

그날 티셰프만이 티밥을 제공하는 데 일조한 것은 아니다. 결제 과정을 도와준 T1 동료, 정작 자신들은 식사도 제대로 못 하고 땀 흘리며 여기저기 뛰어다니던 그들의 모습이 떠오른다.

핫도그 제공 작전의 개시에 앞서 "얼굴이 새카맣게 타도 씩 웃으며 행사를 무사히 마치겠다" 다짐하던 한 직원의 모습이 기억에 남는다. 소중한 동료가 없었다면 절대로 해낼 수 없었던 미션이다. 감사하고 감사하다. 2025년 다시 열릴 홈그라운드를 위해 오늘의 경험을 소중히 간직하며, 앞으로 더욱 철저하게 준비해나갈 것이다.

About the Dish

American-style hot dogs are a quintessential street food in the U.S., typically consisting of a sausage tucked into a long bun, dressed with ketchup, mustard, pickle relish, and other toppings. Easy to eat on the go, they are popular at baseball games, festivals, and various outdoor events. Different regions and vendors experiment with diverse toppings and styles, offering endless variations on this classic treat.

음식 소개

미국식 핫도그는 길쭉한 번 사이에 소시지를 끼우고 케첩, 머스터드, 피클 렐리시 등을 곁들여 먹는 대표적인 미국 길거리 음식이다. 손쉽게 들고 먹을 수 있어 야구장이나 축제 현장 등에서 인기가 있으며, 지역별로 다양한 토핑 조합과 스타일로 즐길 수 있다.

RECIPE

 Hot Dog Bun(40g) : 5　　　　핫도그빵(40g) 5개

Plain Hot Dog
Sausage : 1(84g)
Relish : 50g / Onion : 20g
Ketchup : 15g / Mustard : 15g

플레인 핫도그
소시지 1개(84g)
렐리쉬 50g / 양파 20g
케첩 15g / 머스터드 15g

Chili Hot Dog
Sausage : 1(84g)
Relish : 50g / Onion : 20g
Chili Sauce : 20g

칠리 핫도그
소시지 1개(84g)
렐리쉬 50g / 양파 20g
칠리소스 20g

Garlic Hot Dog
Sausage : 1(84g)
Relish : 50g / Onion : 20g
Garlic Dipping Sauce : 20g
Garlic Flakes : 3g

갈릭 핫도그
소시지 1개(84g)
렐리쉬 50g / 양파 20g
갈릭디핑소스 20g
마늘후레이크 3g

Ham Salad Hot Dog
Onion : 20g
Sandwich Ham : 20g
Boiled Egg : 50g
Cucumber : 20g
Sweet Corn : 50g
Mayonnaise : 50g

햄샐러드 핫도그
양파 20g
샌드위치용햄 20g
삶은계란 50g
오이 20g
스위트콘 50g
마요네즈 50g

Tuna Salad Hot Dog
Onion : 20g
Tuna : 60g
Boiled Egg : 50g
Cucumber : 20g
Sweet Corn : 50g
Mayonnaise : 50g

참치샐러드 핫도그
양파 20g
참치 60g
삶은계란 50g
오이 20g
스위트콘 50g
마요네즈 50g

 **Tip**

- Adding sauteed onions enhances the onion flavor.
- When cooking the sausage, adding oil to the pan ensures the sausage retains its juices.
- You can also use coleslaw, pumpkin salad, or sweet potato salad.

- 볶은 양파를 넣으면 양파 풍미를 더 느낄 수 있다.
- 소시지를 익힐 때 팬에 기름을 넣고 돌려가면서 구우면 소시지 육즙이 더 잘 유지된다.
- 코울슬로, 단호박 샐러드, 고구마 샐러드를 활용할 수도 있다.

PREPARATION

1 Chop the onion into 0.5cm pieces.

양파를 0.5cm 크기로 다져준다.

2 Chop the cucumber into 0.3cm pieces, add a little salt, mix, and drain.

오이를 0.3cm 크기로 다져준 후 소금을 약간 넣고 버무린 후 물기를 빼준다.

3 Drain the sweet corn at this time.

이때 스위트콘도 물기를 빼준다.

4 Drain the oil from the canned tuna.

캔참치도 기름을 빼준다.

5 Boil the sausage in water for about 3 minutes.

소시지를 끓는 물에 3분간 데쳐준다.

6 Mash the boiled egg whole.

삶은 계란을 통으로 으깬다.

7 Mix the salad ingredients.

샐러드 재료를 버무려준다.

COOKING STEPS

1 **Plain Hot Dog** ❶ Add the sausage ❷ Add the onion and relish ❸ Drizzle the sauce.

플레인핫도그 ❶ 소시지 넣기 ❷ 양파와 렐리시 넣기 ❸ 소스 뿌리기.

2 **Chili Hot Dog** ❶ Add the sausage ❷ Add the onion and relish ❸ Drizzle with chili sauce.

칠리핫도그 ❶ 소시지 넣기 ❷ 양파와 렐리시 넣기 ❸ 칠리소스 뿌리기.

③ Garlic Hot Dog ❶ Add the sausage ❷ Add the onion ❸ Drizzle garlic dipping sauce in a zigzag pattern ❹ Sprinkle with garlic flakes.

갈릭핫도그 ❶ 소시지 넣기 ❷ 양파 넣기 ❸ 갈릭디핑소스 지그재그로 뿌리기 ❹ 마늘 후레이크 뿌리기.

④ Ham Salad Hot Dog ❶ Add the ham ❷ Add the boiled eggs ❸ Add the salad mix ❹ Sprinkle parsley on top.

햄샐러드 핫도그 ❶ 햄 넣기 ❷ 삶은 계란 넣기 ❸ 샐러드믹스 넣기 ❹ 파슬리 뿌리기.

5 **Tuna Salad Hot Dog** ❶ Mix the salad greens with drained tuna ❷ Open the bread and add the tuna salad ❸ Sprinkle parsley on top.

참치샐러드 핫도그 ❶ 샐러드 믹스에 기름을 뺀 참치를 넣고 버무리기 ❷ 빵을 벌려 참치샐러드 넣기 ❸ 파슬리 뿌리기.

Episode 14

Jeukseoktteokbokki

Special Meal for the Entire T1 Family Who Joined the Home Ground Game

즉석 떡볶이 – 홈그라운드 경기를 함께 한 T1 가족 전체 특식

Date July 11, 2024
Introduction The start of the scorching summer of 2024. Introducing a special meal prepared for everyone at T1 who came together at the T1 home ground.
Allergen Information 🥚 Egg, 🌾 Wheat
Spiciness Level 🌶️ Spicy (Similar to Shin Ramyun)
Way to Cook 🍲 Simmering

일자 2024. 7. 11
소개 2024년 뜨거웠던 여름의 시작. T1 홈그라운드에서 함께한 T1인 모두를 위한 전체 특식을 소개한다.
알러지 정보 계란, 밀
맵기 단계 신라면
조리 기법 부글부글 끓이기

RECIPE

 Ingredients(for 4 Servings)

Tteokbokki Tteok : 360g	떡볶이떡 360g
Eggs : 2	달걀 2개
Sausages : 3	소시지 3개
Jjolmyeon Noodles : 100g	쫄면사리 100g
Square Fish Cake : 100g	사각어묵 100g
Ramen Noodles : 0.5	라면사리 0.5개
Green Onion : 100g	대파 100g
Cabbage : 200g	양배추 200g
Carrot : 30g	당근 30g
Onion : 150g	양파 150g
Water : 4 cups(800ml)	물 4컵(800ml)

재료(4인분)

 Sauce — 소스

Gochujang : 140g	고추장 140g
Chunjang : 40g	춘장 40g
Sugar : 160g	설탕 160g
Fine Red Pepper Powder : 30g	고운 고춧가루 30g
Coarse Red Pepper Powder : 60g	굵은 고춧가루 60g
Light Soy Sauce : 90ml	진간장 90ml
Water : 1 cup(180ml)	물 1컵(180ml)

 Tools — 도구

Jeongol Pot(Wide Pot) — 전골냄비

 Tip

- Adding seafood enhances the dish with a refreshing and light flavor.
- Reversing the ratio of gochujang and red pepper powder turns it into soupy tteokbokki.
- Eat the noodles first to prevent the broth from reducing too much.
- Use the leftover broth to make fried rice by adding chopped kimchi, seaweed flakes, and sesame oil.

- 해산물을 넣으면 시원하고 담백한 맛을 느낄 수 있다.
- 고추장과 고춧가루 비율을 반대로 바꾸면 국물떡볶이가 된다.
- 면류를 먼저 먹어야 국물이 완전히 쫄지 않는다.
- 먹고 남은 국물에 다진 김치, 김가루, 참기름을 넣고 볶음밥을 해먹자.

PREPARATION

1 Cut the green onion diagonally into 1cm lengths.

대파를 1cm 길이로 어슷썬다.

2 Slice the cabbage into pieces 3cm thick and 4cm long.

양배추를 두께 3cm, 길이 4cm로 썬다.

3 Cut the Fish Cake into 5cm-long strips.

어묵을 5cm 길이로 썬다.

④ Slice the onions and carrots into 0.5cm thick pieces.

양파와 당근을 0.5cm 두께로 썬다.

⑤ Mix the gochujang, chunjang, sugar, fine red pepper powder, coarse red pepper powder, soy sauce, and water to make the sauce.

고추장, 춘장, 설탕, 고운 고춧가루, 굵은 고춧가루, 진간장, 물을 잘 섞어 소스를 만든다.

COOKING STEPS

1 Boil eggs for 12 minutes with salt and vinegar to make hard-boiled eggs. After boiling, soak them in cold water, peel the shells, and cut them in half.

소금, 식초를 넣고 12분 동안 삶아 완숙 계란을 만든다. 삶고 나서 찬 물에 담근 후 깐다. 그후 반을 가른다.

2 Prepare a jeongol pot. Arrange vegetables, fish cakes, and sausages along the edges. Place the tteok in the center and lay ramen noodles on top.

전골냄비를 준비해서 가장자리에 야채, 어묵, 소시지를 깔아주고, 떡을 가운데, 라면을 그 위에 놓는다.

3 Add the sauce in the middle, pour in water, and bring it to a boil over high heat.

양념장을 가운데 얹고, 물을 부은 후 강불로 끓인다.

4 Once the broth starts boiling, stir it well with a spatula to prevent sticking. Lower the heat to medium and add jjolmyeon.

국물이 끓기 시작하면 눌러붙지 않게 주걱으로 잘 저으며 중불로 줄인 후 쫄면을 넣어준다.

5 Since the noodles and jjolmyeon cook quickly, reduce the heat to low and finish cooking.

면과 쫄면은 금방 익으므로 약불로 줄인 후, 마무리한다.

Episode 15

Cheese Tonkatsu

What Did Untara Want to Eat Before His Military Enlistment?

치즈돈까스 – 운타라 선수가 군입대 전 먹고 싶었던 음식은 과연?

Date — Dec 8, 2020
Introduction — Let's revisit the cheese tonkatsu, a dish introduced in 2022 to bid farewell to Untara before his enlistment.
Allergen Information — 🥛 Milk, 🥚 Egg, 🌾 Wheat, 🐖 Pork
Spiciness Level — 🌶 Mild
Way to Cook — Deep-frying

일자 — 2020. 12. 8
소개 — 2022년, 운타라 선수의 입대를 아쉬워하며 선보인 치즈돈까스를 만나보자.
알러지 정보 — 우유, 계란, 밀, 돼지고기
맵기 단계 — 순한맛
조리 기법 — 튀김

STORY

When I first joined T1, the very first person I met was streamer Untara. At the time, he wasn't officially part of T1's roster, so our initial encounter was a brief exchange of greetings at the cafeteria. Despite this, that first meeting remains vivid in my memory. When I later heard he was joining T1A as an instructor, I was thrilled to reconnect with him.

Untara, who played as T1's top laner for about a year and a half starting in 2017, is now a well-loved streamer. He's known for his witty broadcasting style and insightful commentary, but also for his serious and disciplined teaching approach. His dedication and passion are what make his students so eager to learn under his guidance. T1A is more than a training facility—it's a unique space where aspiring pro players and casual gamers alike can benefit from the expertise of T1 veterans.

내가 T1에 입사했을 때 가장 먼저 만난 사람은 스트리머 운타라 님이다. 당시에는 소속 스트리머가 아니라서, 식사를 하러 식당에 들렀을 때 가볍게 인사를 나눈 정도였지만, 첫 만남은 지금까지도 선명하다. T1A 강사로 합류한다는 소식을 들었을 때, 그때의 반가움이 다시 밀려왔다.

운타라 님은 현역 시절 2017년부터 약 1년 반 동안 T1에서 탑 라이너로 활약했으며, 지금은 스트리머로 활동 중이다. 개인 방송에서의 유쾌한 진행과 매끄러운 해설로도 유명하지만 한편으로는 진지하고 엄격한 강의 스타일로도 잘 알려져 있다. 수강생들이 더욱 열심히 따라가는 이유도 바로 그 진심과 열정 덕분일 것이다.

Park 'Untara' Ui-jin
'운타라' 박의진

The opportunity to learn and have fun simultaneously is what makes it so special. Personally, I've often dreamed of attending one of Untara's lectures at T1A, but my busy schedule has always kept me from doing so. About a year into his role as a T1A instructor, Untara received his military enlistment notice. The news saddened me, and I wanted to prepare something special for him before he left. I remembered how much he enjoyed cheese tonkatsu during our first meeting, so I decided to make it for him myself. I bought some fresh pork from a nearby market, pounded it thin, and wrapped it around a large block of cheese before frying it to golden perfection.

T1A는 단순히 게임 실력을 키우는 곳을 넘어, T1 출신 선배들의 경험과 노하우를 공유받을 수 있는 특별한 공간이다. 프로 선수를 지망하는 학생뿐 아니라 취미로 게임을 즐기려는 사람들에게도 배움과 즐거움을 동시에 선사한다는 점에서 정말 멋지다고 생각한다. 나도 언젠가 시간을 내어 T1A에서 운타라 님께 강의를 받고 싶다는 생각을 자주 한다. 그러나 매번 해야 할 일들에 쫓겨 다음을 기약할 수밖에 없었다. T1A 강사로 1년 정도 활약할 때쯤 운타라 님 앞으로 입영 통지가 날아왔다.

"I never imagined I'd get to eat something like this before enlisting. Thank you," he said, and I replied, "If you visit during your leave, I'll make you something delicious again!" Hoping for his safe return, I even shared a few of my own stories from my time as a military cook. Time flew by after we parted ways. Before I knew it, Untara was discharged and back as T1's streamer.

아쉬운 마음이 들었다. 뭔가 특별한 선물을 하고 싶었다. 첫 만남 때 치즈돈까스를 맛있게 드시던 일이 떠올랐다. 그래서 내가 직접 치즈돈까스를 만들어 드리기로 했다. 가까운 마트에서 고기를 사와 망치로 두드리고 큼직한 치즈 한 덩어리를 속에 넣어 돌돌 말았다. "군대 가기 전에 이런 음식을 먹을 줄은 몰랐어요. 고맙습니다.", "휴가 때 오시면 또 맛있는 거 해드릴게요!"라며 나는 응원했다. 부디 건강하게 돌아오길 바라는 마음을 담아, 취사병 시절 이야기도 살짝 꺼내들었다.
아쉬운 마음으로 보냈 건만 시간이 참 빠르다. 운타라 님은 전역 후 다시 T1의 스트리머로 돌아왔다.

Recently, he joined the T1 League of Legends team in Paris for an event, delighting fans with his cheerful energy and camaraderie. Watching his journey unfold on a global stage, I felt an even deeper appreciation for that first meeting and the memory of sharing cheese tonkatsu. Under the T1 name, all of us are creating new memories and taking on fresh challenges in our own ways. My bond with Untara and every member of T1 is something I truly treasure. It feels like there are even greater stories ahead, waiting to be told through T1 and, of course, TBap.

최근에 열린 파리 행사에서 T1 LoL팀 선수들과 함께 유쾌한 모습을 보여주며 팬들에게 또 다른 즐거움을 선사했다. 전 세계를 무대로 T1과 함께하는 운타라 님의 활약을 보며, 그 특별했던 첫 만남과 치즈돈까스의 추억이 더욱 소중하게 느껴졌다. T1이라는 이름 아래, 우리는 각자의 자리에서 새로운 추억과 도전을 이어가고 있다. 운타라 님과의 인연도, T1 구성원 한 명 한 명과의 인연도, 나에게는 더 각별하다. 앞으로 더 멋진 티밥으로 멋진 이야기가 펼쳐질 것 같은 기분이 든다.

About the Dish

Cheese tonkatsu is a variation of the traditional pork cutlet, where a thinly pounded piece of pork is rolled with cheese inside before being breaded and deep-fried. The crispy outer crust and the gooey, savory cheese create an irresistibly rich flavor and texture. Popular in Korean and Japanese eateries, cheese tonkatsu pairs well with a sweet sauce or a fresh salad, enhancing its delicious taste.

음식 소개

치즈돈까스는 얇게 펴낸 돼지고기에 치즈를 넣어 튀겨낸 변형 돈까스다. 바삭한 튀김옷 안에 녹아내리는 치즈가 고소한 풍미를 더해 더욱 풍부한 식감을 선사한다. 한국과 일본식 식당에서 인기 있는 메뉴로, 달콤한 소스나 샐러드와 함께 즐기면 맛이 한층 살아난다.

RECIPE

Ingredients (for 2 Servings)

Pork Tenderloin : 240g	돼지 등심 240g
Mozzarella Block Cheese : 160g	모짜블록 치즈 160g
Salt : a little	소금 약간
Pepper : a little	후추 약간
Flour : 90g	밀가루 90g
Eggs : 2	계란 2개
Japanese Bread Crumbs : 180g	일식빵가루 180g
Cooking Oil : 360ml	식용유 360g
Parsley : a little	파슬리 약간

Sauce — 소스

Water : 100ml	물 100ml
Onion : 0.5	양파 0.5개
Celery : 0.5	샐러리 0.5개
Bay Leaves : 3	월계수잎 3장
Worcestershire Sauce : 40ml	우스타소스 40ml
Soy Sauce : 20ml	간장 20ml
Tomato Ketchup : 30ml	토마토케첩 30ml
Sugar : 3 tbsps	설탕 3큰술
Starch(Water) : 0.5 tbsps(1 tbsp)	전분(물) 0.5큰술(1큰술)

Tools — 도구

Plate	접시
Meat Mallet	조리용 망치
Draining Tray	돈까스용 드레인

Tip

- If you don't have a meat mallet, you can make shallow cuts in the meat.
- Using smaller pieces of block cheese will give you a round-shaped cheese tonkatsu.
- You can also use shredded mozzarella cheese instead of block cheese.
- If you flatten chicken breast and use the same method, you can make a cheese chicken katsu.

- 고기를 펴는 망치가 없다면 칼집을 내자.
- 블록 치즈 크기를 작게 만들면 동그란 치즈돈까스를 맛볼 수 있다.
- 블록 치즈 대신 피자 치즈를 사용해도 무방하다.
- 닭가슴살을 넓게 핀 다음 똑같은 방식으로 치즈를 넣고 반죽하면 치즈치킨까스가 된다.

PREPARATION

1 Pat the pork loin dry with a paper towel to remove excess blood.

키친타월로 돼지 등심 핏물을 뺀다.

2 Place plastic wrap on a cutting board, then place the pork on top. Cover the pork with more plastic wrap and use a mallet to flatten the meat, making it thin and wide.

도마에 비닐을 깔고 그 위에 고기를 올린 다음, 비닐로 고기를 덮고 망치로 고기를 얇고 넓게 편다.

3 Sprinkle with salt and pepper.

소금, 후추를 뿌려준다.

4 Slice the block cheese into 2cm thick sticks.

블록 치즈를 2cm 두께 막대 모양으로 썰어준다.

5 Slice the onion and celery into 0.1cm thick pieces.

양파와 샐러리를 0.1cm로 썬다.

6 Combine bay leaves, Worcestershire sauce, soy sauce, water, ketchup, and sugar. Bring the mixture to a boil, then thicken with starch.

월계수잎, 우스터소스, 간장, 물, 토마토케첩, 설탕을 잘 섞어서 끓이고 전분으로 농도를 잡아준다.

COOKING STEPS

1 Place one block of cheese on the seasoned meat that has been flattened. Roll it up tightly to ensure there are no gaps.

고기 위에 블록 치즈를 하나 놓고 돌돌 말아준다.

2 Wrap the meat with cheese in a wrap to secure it, then refrigerate for 10 minutes.

치즈를 품은 고기를 랩으로 감싸 고정시킨 후, 10분간 냉장 숙성시킨다.

3 Take out the refrigerated meat and coat it with flour, egg, and breadcrumbs in that order.

냉장 숙성시킨 고기를 꺼내어 밀가루, 계란, 빵가루 순으로 묻힌다.

4 Heat the oil to 160°C and fry the meat for about 4 minutes and 30 seconds.

기름 온도를 160도로 맞춘 후 4분 30초 동안 튀겨준다.

5 Mix the sauce and boil it, then adjust the thickness with starch water.

소스를 섞어서 끓여주다가 전분물로 농도를 맞춰준다.

6 Cut the fried pork cutlet in half.

튀긴 돈까스를 반으로 커팅한다.

7 Set it with the cheese side up, and garnish with parsley for plating.

치즈가 위로 가도록 세팅한 후에 파슬리를 뿌려 플레이팅한다.

Recommendation

I really enjoy malatang. I think this is a great opportunity for you all to try making it yourself using the recipes in the book. Enjoy!
_ Lee 'Faker' Sang-hyeok

I love Jangeodeopbap(Grilled Eel Rice Bowl). When I came to T1, the chefs prepared it for me and I was deeply moved. The recipe for that Jangeodeopbap is in the book. Everyone, let's cook!
_ Choi 'Doran' Hyeon-joon

I brag about the chef's special dishes on social media whenever I get the chance, especially the Samgyetang, which restored my energy last year. I hope you'll follow the recipe, make it, and stay strong! It's good!
_ Lee 'Gumayusi' Min-hyeong

This book reminded me of the last Cheese Tonkatsu I ate before I enlisted. The story that the chef had carefully crafted for me on that plate was more than a meal, it was a deeply felt affection. Already, I find myself sitting at the table in T1 again after my enlistment. It's a precious book that made me feel nostalgic for the past and excited for the future at the same time.
_ Park 'Untara' Ui-jin

For me, as a founding member of T1, it's a team that holds special emotions to this day, so the food has special meaning too. The book is full of anecdotes that give you an intimate look into the T1 family's eating life, including memories of the day they made Tteokguk. The book is easy to follow, even for beginners, and you can share in the spirit of the team. Highly recommended.
_ Lim 'BoxeR' Yo-hwan

'The steak and ragu pasta were special dishes just for my partner, Bang, and me...' I still remember the taste. We're happy to share the happiness and excitement we felt with readers of this book. The 'family' atmosphere of T1 is reflected in the recipes and stories in this book.
_ Lee 'Wolf' Jae-wan

Meal times are some of my most cherished memories at T1. When I decided to retire, the steak and pasta you cooked for me and Wolf was an emotional moment, and the gratitude I felt and the warmth of the team is all captured in this book. I hope fans will enjoy it and experience for themselves how wonderful it is that the passion for e-sports and team culture lives on through food.
_ Bae 'Bang' Jun-sik

T1's Circus runs on the power of hearty meals. The key ingredient is undoubtedly Chef's love and magic touch.
_ T1 COO Josh Ahn

The T1 Cafeteria and T1 Bap have been a part of T1's history. The food that T1's athletes and staff ate on their way to the esports crown is in this book. Looking through this book, you'll realize that the hearty 'Bap' was T1's secret weapon in their rise to the top.
_ T1 Kang Min-jung

Congratulations on the publication of your book, Chef. I've always admired your passion and personality, and this book is the culmination of that passion. Cooking is an art that reflects a chef's philosophy and personality, and I'm sure you will set a new standard in this book. I'm sure your readers will find new inspiration in your unique style. I hope this book will be a favorite for many years to come.
_ T1 Member

이 책을 추천합니다

마라탕을 즐겨 먹어서 이번에 셰프님께서 준비하는 책을 통해 많은 분들이 레시피를 보고 직접 요리해 먹을 수 있는 좋은 기회라고 생각합니다. 다들 맛있게 드세요.
_ '페이커' 이상혁 선수

제가 장어덮밥을 좋아하는데, T1에 와서 셰프님들이 준비해주신 덕분에 감동받았습니다. 그때 먹었던 장어덮밥 레시피가 책에 담겨 있습니다. 다들 한 번 해드셨으면 좋겠습니다.
_ '도란' 최현준 선수

기회가 될 때마다 특식을 개인 SNS를 통해 티밥을 자랑합니다. 특히 이번 여름에 삼계탕을 먹고 힘이 났던 기억이 새록하네요. 팬 여러분도 레시피를 따라서 만들어드시고 힘내셨으면 합니다.
_ '구마유시' 이민형 선수

이 책을 보니 제가 군 입대 전 마지막으로 맛본 치즈돈까스가 떠오릅니다. 셰프님이 정성스레 만들어주신 음식 한 접시에 담긴 이야기는 그저 '한 끼 식사'를 넘어 마음 깊이 와닿았습니다. 벌써 전역 후 다시 T1 식탁에 앉아 있는 저를 발견합니다. 과거의 추억과 미래의 기대를 동시에 품게 해주는 귀한 책입니다.
_ '운타라' 박의진

제게 있어서 T1은 창단 멤버로서 시작부터 함께해온 남다른 감성이 있는 팀입니다. 그만큼 음식에도 특별한 의미가 담겨 있죠. 이 책에는 떡국을 끓였던 날의 추억을 포함해 T1 패밀리의 생활을 간접적으로 느낄 수 있는 에피소드가 가득합니다. 요리 초보라 할지라도 쉽게 따라 할 수 있고, 팀의 정신을 함께 공감할 수 있는 이 책을 강력 추천드립니다.
_ '박서' 임요환

'뱅이랑 저에게 맞춰 준비된 스테이크와 라구 파스타…' 그 맛의 기억은 아직도 생생합니다. 이 책을 통해 독자분들도 저희가 느꼈던 행복과 감동을 같이 누릴 수 있을 거라 생각하니 벌써부터 설레네요. T1이 가진 '가족 같은' 분위기가 책에 담긴 레시피와 스토리를 통해서 고스란히 전해집니다.
_ '울프' 이재완

T1에서 함께하며 가장 값진 추억 중 하나가 바로 식사 시간이었습니다. 은퇴를 결심했을 때, 저와 울프에게 정성껏 차려주신 스테이크와 파스타는 정말 감동이었죠. 이 책에는 그때 느꼈던 고마움과 팀의 따뜻한 분위기가 모두 녹아 있습니다. e스포츠에 대한 열정과 팀 문화를 요리로 풀어낸다는 게 얼마나 대단한 일인지, 독자 여러분도 꼭 한번 맛보셨으면 좋겠습니다.
_ '뱅' 배준식

T1 서커스는 밥심으로부터 나오고, 그 핵심 재료는 단연 김재형 셰프님의 사랑과 손맛입니다.
_ T1 COO 안웅기

T1의 역사와 언제나 함께 했던 T1 카페테리아 T1 Bap. T1의 선수들과 임직원들이 e스포츠 왕관을 차지하기 위해 먹은 음식들이 책에 등장합니다. 우리를 최고의 자리에 있게 한 시크릿 웨폰이 정성 가득한 '밥'이었다는 걸 알 수 있을 것입니다.
_ T1 강민정

책 출간을 축하드립니다. 이 책은 셰프님의 열정이 모인 결정체라고 생각합니다. 요리는 셰프의 철학과 개성이 반영되는 예술이고, 이 책을 통해 셰프님께서 새로운 요리의 기준을 제시하실 거라 확신합니다. 독자분들도 셰프님의 특별함에서 새로운 영감을 얻으실 거라 믿습니다. 이 책이 오랫동안 많은 분의 애장서가 되길 바랍니다. 앞으로도 멋진 활약 기대하겠습니다!
_ T1 동료

TBap, T1's Dining Table : TChef's TBap Tier List for T1(English And Korean Edition)
티밥, T1의 밥상 : T1을 위한 티셰프의 티밥 티어리스트(영한 에디션)

1판 1쇄 발행 2025년 04월 01일

지은이 김재형
상표제공 에스케이텔레콤씨에스티원 주식회사
영문 김정현

펴낸이 최현우 · **기획** 버즈 · **편집** 박현규, 김성경, 최혜민
디자인 nu:n
마케팅 오힘찬 · **피플** 최순주
펴낸곳 골든래빗(주)
등록 2020년 7월 7일 제 2020-000183호
주소 서울 마포구 양화로 186 LC타워 5층 514호
전화 0505-398-0505 · **팩스** 0505-537-0505
이메일 ask@goldenrabbit.co.kr
홈페이지 www.goldenrabbit.co.kr
SNS facebook.com/goldenrabbit2020
ISBN 979-11-94383-07-9 03590(무선)
ISBN 979-11-94383-08-6 03590(양장)
* 파본은 구입한 서점에서 바꿔드립니다.

우리는 가치가 성장하는 시간을 만듭니다.
골든래빗은 가치가 성장하는 도서를 함께 만드실 저자님을 찾고 있습니다.
내가 할 수 있을까 망설이는 대신, 용기 내어 골든래빗의 문을 두드려보세요.
apply@goldenrabbit.co.kr

이 책은 대한민국 저작권법의 보호를 받습니다.
일부를 인용 또는 재사용하려면 반드시 저자와 골든래빗(주)의 동의를 구해야 합니다.

골든래빗
바로가기